THE

PRAYER THAT TEACHES
TO PRAY.

BY THE REV.

MARCUS DODS. M.A., D.D.,

*Author of " Israel's Iron Age," " The Book of Genesis," " The
Parables of Our Lord," etc.*

FLEMING H. REVELL COMPANY,

NEW YORK.   CHICAGO.   TORONTO.

Publishers of Evangelical Literature.

CONTENTS.

After this manner therefore pray ye: Our Father, which art in heaven, Hallowed be thy name. Thy kingdom come. Thy will be done in earth, as it is in heaven. Give us this day our daily bread. And forgive us our debts, as we forgive our debtors. And lead us not into temptation; but deliver us from evil: For thine is the kingdom, and the power, and the glory, for ever. Amen.—Matt. vi. 9–13.

1.

" After this manner therefore pray ye: Our Father which
art in heaven."

FAR better than all instructions and precepts
about prayer is this simple model.   Using this,
we learn both how to pray and what to pray for.
And when we have learned this prayer, it will be
time to consider how we shall expand the teaching of our Lord.   If it is "after this manner" we
are to pray, then who can restrain prayer on the
ground of lack of time for devotion ?   This is the
" five words with understanding" preferable to ten
thousand of formality or repetition.   Here is no
vain and heathenish babbling, as if the length
of our prayer were to measure the value of its
answer ; nor anv explanatory repetition, as if God

did not know what things we have need of. But there is here only a straightforward laying before God of one desire after another. Simplicity and brevity are discernible at a glance, and are taught at the first lesson.

But if it is "after this manner" we are to pray, then who can restrain prayer on the ground of mental inability to pray? For here are desires presented before God with the barest possible clothing of words. Elaborate language, then, is no essential of prayer; nor yet ingenious thought, nor the observant penetration of spirit which discovers the minute or hidden wants of man. Only so much language is required as makes the desire audible. We are backward in prayer, not because it is too difficult, but because it is too simple for us. It is so unlike our other ways of gaining and getting, that we are always trying to make it something more than it is, an asking for what we want. And to every man this model prayer says, "If you want nothing from God, then do not pray—you cannot pray; but whatever you want from Him, ask for, and you pray."

This prayer, however, is a model as much for its matter as its manner. So that we ought not only to imitate, but use it. We are not to be satisfied if our prayers have some general resemblance to it, but we are to use the very words taught us by our Lord. Does some one think that it may do well enough for beginners, or for ordinary occasions, or to eke out some petitions of our own devising, but that an advanced spiritual condition demands something fuller and richer? So apparently thought one of our Lord's disciples, for we read in the narrative of Luke that, when the disciples saw Christ pray, one of them asked to be taught to pray; hoping, probably, to receive some fuller, more striking, more sublime petitions. But what says our Lord? Not only, as here, "After this manner pray ye;" but, "when ye pray, *say.*" And there is no getting past the evident precept here delivered, that we ought habitually to use these words. And as we use them, we shall find that though we learnt them at our mother's knee, it takes a lifetime to fill them with their meaning, and eternity to give them all their answer. If these be our leading and guiding desires, it matters less what else we are seeking. But if these be not at all among our desires, then we are not being led in the best direction, and have yet to learn what these petitions include, and how desirable their contents are. To let this prayer lie

with all the riches of its promise in our view, and
not to use it, is to be cruel to our own souls as
Saul was to his men, when he commanded that
none should put forth his hand to take of the
honey that was dripping from the trees of the
wood, which taken would enlighten the eyes and
give strength to the faint. Are we anxious to
know what future lies before us ? Let us pray
this prayer and we become prophets of our own
future, surely knowing that these are the things
which shall be ; for by commanding us so to pray,
our Lord has given us sure pledge of the fulfil-
ment of these things. Here, then, we have the
future of the Church, the future of those on whom
God delights to show the wealth of His love. We
have it here, as it lies now in the desires of those
who are tending towards it through the unlikely
and unpromising things of this world. And if
with one heart and mind we were desiring these
things, would they not be more speedily accomplished, the obstructions of the world sooner con-
quered, and our own blessedness and triumph in
God more rapidly achieved ? This prayer, taught
by our Lord, and wrought by His Spirit in the
desires of His people, is the bond of attraction
drawing earth steadily towards heaven ; drawing

it with a momentum ever increasing as the distance becomes less, and as these common desires
find a hold in a greater number of hearts.

Of the arrangement of this prayer many things
have been noticed—some fanciful, some just.   It
has been compared to the law of the Decalogue,
inasmuch as, like it, this prayer has two tables,
the first pertaining to the things of God, the
second to the things of man.   There has also been
noticed (if not with more justice, at least with
more meaning) a reference to the Trinity throughout; the first petition of either part of the prayer
referring to God as Creator and Preserver; the
second petition of either part referring to God as
Redeemer; and the third to God the Holy Spirit.
This has considerable foundation in the form of
the prayer, and not a little significance with regard to the completeness of the blessing we should
seek.   But the obvious division is the useful one
to bear in mind.   There are two parts.   In the
first part the object of worship rivets the thought
that has been turned towards Him, and those desires which concern His great purposes are first
uttered; and only after that follows the second
part, in which the attention turns to our own condition and wants.   The petitions of the first part

are inseparable from one another; each includes the one which follows; the name of God must be recognised and hallowed before His kingdom can be established, and only when His kingdom has come can His will be done. And, indeed, all these petitions are included in the very invocation, when we say, "Our Father which art in heaven;" for when we say this with our hearts, we already hallow the name, own the authority, and submit to the will of God. And, again, the first part of the prayer paves the way for the second, and introduces it; for the things which we implore in the first part are not to come to pass irrespective of our condition. We are men; if, then, the will of God is to be done by us on earth, we must be maintained in life. We are sinners; if, then, His kingdom is to come to us, our sins must be forgiven, since nothing that defiles can enter that kingdom. If all the petitions of the first part are to be answered, and if our calling God "Father" is not to be in word only, then we must depend on God to give us the guidance of His wisdom, and to rescue us from the power of the Evil.

Let us try, then, to learn what is contained in this invocation, and to see how it implies every good disposition for prayer, and includes every

encouragement, remembering that as much that
we say is determined by the tone, and that as
some words in our common speech, such as
"mother," "father," are peculiarly elastic, con-
taining as much meaning as the heart which uses
them can pour into them, so we have to learn to
give to these words, "Our Father," the tone of
Christ; and as we learn this, we shall find that
we never do fill them to the full, that they rather
still extend beyond our actual feelings, and show
us that there is more to be striven after. Indeed,
if there be any who thinks he has exhausted
these words, who has never trembled at the glory
and the promise that are in them, who has never
hesitated, even on his knees, before he has dared
to take them and use them as his words, is not
he still using them merely as a form, not believing, perhaps never having even conceived, that
there is a reality which they depict?

The first thing to be noticed about these words
is, that they are new in the Bible and in the
world, put now for the first time into the mouth
of man. They begin New-Testament prayer.
They evidence that a change is passing; that as
men are now expected to *be* more than formerly,
having clearer declarations of the will of God, so

they are invited to richer encouragement, having clearer exhibition of the nature of God. " The true light now shineth." God has passed through the clouds and darkness that are around His throne, and has dwelt with us, that we might " acquaint ourselves with God." What was given long before as a promise, "Thou shalt call me My Father," is now fulfilled. In all the fervent confidence of David we never find him uttering these words, " My Father." And wherever we do find God spoken of as the Father of Israel, this title seems to refer to the kindness of God as their guide and defence, or to His creating and preserving power. Thus Malachi explains the cause, " Have we not all one Father?" by " Hath not one God created us?" And even in this sense we do not find it used in the form of address. The nearest approach to it that we find is that most moving prayer recorded in Isaiah, in which the orphaned and desolate people reassure themselves of God's favour in these words, "Doubtless thou art our Father, our Redeemer;" but by the last part of the same supplication we see that little more is meant even here than to call upon God as a faithful Creator, who has indeed entered into some peculiar connexion with them, for it is said, "Thou, O Lord, art our Father; we are the clay, and thou our potter, and we are all the work of thy hand!" In this there is a dimness which the birth of Immanuel scatters. There is a feeling after the indissoluble bond, but in the humanity of our Lord we see the union formed. It was for Christ the Son to give us this liberty of calling God "our Father."

So that there is something more here than the mere acknowledgment of God as our Creator and Keeper. There is a recognition, distinct and necessary, of the Son of God and His work, and through Him we aspire to an intimacy which the Creator has not with any mere creature. By Christ we are lifted to quite a new level and rank before God. We still have God as our faithful Creator, who will supply all our necessities. The Creator is included in the Father; but in the Father we have, over and above, the assurance that our connexion with Him is one of love and of lasting relationship; that we shall not be suffered to go adrift, but shall be brought up into His likeness, and shall live with Him; and that the ground on which this relationship is established is one of unutterable dignity, the Son of God having become our brother, our nature being

now worn by the same person as wears the nature
of God. If, therefore, we do not acknowledge
Christ in saying, "Our Father," this epithet is
either profane, misty, or heathenish. The heathen
called God Father, seeing the goodness, but not
understanding the majesty, of Him on whom they
called. And there is among ourselves a confused
idea of the love of God, and of His desire to bless
us, which seems to justify our calling God, as by
a figure, "Our Father." But it is no such confused and delusive figure that Christ sets before
us, but a reality. It is a fact accomplished, that
God has become man; a present reality, that God
is man. The Son of God has become Son of Man,
and for this very purpose—"that we might receive
the adoption of sons;" that we might claim the
same Father as Christ claims.

These words, then, which the Son puts into
our lips, again and again raise our hearts to the
belief, that not only may we expect for His sake
many blessings from God, so that it shall be a
very apt simile to call Him Father, but that God
enters into a relationship with us in Him, and becomes for ever connected with us in a way that
secures that all blessings shall be ours. It is not
on account of what we receive from God that we

are to think of Him with filial gratitude, and
count Him a Father; but because He is in very
truth our Father, we shall receive all things at
His hand.   The relationship is to be first in our
minds, deeper also in our affections; and, this
being so, hope will be easy and humility natural.
This is what humbles us and raises us up to believe that God has connected Himself with us.
Supposing that nothing ever came of this relationship, still it must remain, and remain for ever.
Our relationship to God has been established;
the Elder Brother of our race calls God Father;
and irrespective of all that may result from it,
this relationship is satisfying to man.   Our
natures are bound to that of God in the person
of Christ; and so long as that person remains
undestroyed we remain related to God.   There
is, of course, no earthly relationship which fully
sets forth this our connexion with God.   It is a
separate, singular reality, and it must be conceived
of separately in its own reality.   Other relation-
ships may help us to understand it; but while it
is only considered under earthly figures, we are
in danger of forgetting that underneath there lies
the substantial reality of our sonship.   And this,
instead of being less true than earthly relation-

ships, is the one relationship which when a man
enters into he ceases to be homeless and a wan-
derer, a fugitive and vagabond upon the face of
the earth, and from the face of God—ceases to be
a mere withered leaf borne helpless on the wind,
whose origin none cares to trace, and whose des-
tiny none turns to see. He has found his place in
the universe, he has found a hold and a hope ; and
however in himself unstable, weak, and incapable,
he rests enduringly in the unchangeable Father.
He has been outside, thinking the world a strange,
cold, barren, friendless, and unsatisfying place ;
he has wandered about, not seeing " through the
thick cloud," and still less dreaming that One was
seeing and caring for him, and now he finds he
has a Father—One to love, One to serve, One to
glorify, One to worship.*

But is it so sacred a ground as this that we
are to tread in each day's ordinary approach to
God ? No other path is open. The only prayer
our Lord will teach begins, " Our Father." These
words it is easy to use in the figurative sense,

---

* " I looked on my right hand, and beheld, but there was
no man that would know me : refuge failed me ; no man
cared for my soul. I cried unto thee, O Lord : I said, Thou
art my refuge, and my portion in the land of the living."—
Ps. cxlii. 4, 5.

for we can all readily acknowledge that God has been kind, and acted towards us like a Father. But this sense wins us nothing. It goes round, like a thief or a robber, seeking another entrance to the favour of God than the door that He has Himself opened in Christ, and therefore it brings us no nearer God, but only misleads us. And there is no need that we seek for another entrance, for the door is wide enough. It lets in every one that would pass through it. The one thing that we have to show as our passport by this gate is our humanity. If we say that we are born of woman, as Christ was "born of a woman," then His Father owns us. This is all. There is no man who may not use this prayer. And there is no man who is more entitled to use it than another. For the title does not lie in the petitioner, but in Christ. These words do not say, "If you are of kindred spirit with Christ, if you can depend upon the resolves you have made to live a pure and holy life, if you have often used this prayer already, then come, and with freedom and boldness call God Father;" but they go out to the ends of the earth, they look upon all human conditions, they consider the fair and the foul, the stately, noble, and promising in

2

human character, and also all that is wrecked and lost, and they say, " If you are human, if you wear the nature worn by the Son, if you are born of woman, then no matter whatever else you are, come, and say, ' My Father.'"

These words may be abused. A man may shrink from this holy relationship, and yet call upon God. Of course he gains nothing by it ; the favour of God has never been stolen into under cover of deceit. He knows who come to Him through Christ, and who only name the name of Christ. But we may deceive ourselves. And therefore we are to listen to conscience, which tells us that a likeness of character is expected between father and child. This likeness is found in all who call God Father in truth. Such an assimilation Christ supposes, saying, in this same Sermon on the Mount, " Love your enemies, do good to them that hate you, *that ye may be* the children of your Father which is in heaven." But to recognise, own, and call upon our Father is the first and most grateful promise of likeness to Him. And as the earthly parent feels a new bond to his child, when the child, in its first efforts at language, calls upon him and claims him as his father, so the first movement of the Spirit of holiness within the child of God teaches him to cry, " Abba, Father," and, imperfectly though it be spoken, God hails it as the sign of holiness begun, and as the earnest of likeness to Himself.

This same idea is carried out by the epithet attached; for we say not merely, " Our Father," but distinctively, " Our Father which art in heaven." And as the ideas of holiness and power are those which all men naturally associate with " heaven," we are to bear in mind mainly these two things about Him to whom we pray—that He is holy, and that He is powerful. No doubt there are other ideas which are also suggested to our thoughts as these words pass our lips. No doubt, by praying to Heaven, we acknowledge that earth is not sufficient for us; that the things of earth are gifts, not here of themselves, but sent by God, and that " a man can receive nothing, except it be given him of Heaven." We look to Heaven as the source of all power; when the heavens hear the earth, then the earth yields her fruit. This expression helps us further in prayer, by giving to God a distinct habitation. Our prayer would be much more difficult were we permitted to say nothing more than, " Our

Father." Our minds are by far too weak to grasp the idea of an omnipresent spirit. It is true, as it has been said, " Where God is, there is heaven—and where is God not?" But ought we not rather to say, " Whither Christ has ascended, and now lives with His human body, there is heaven, and the presence of the Father for us?" Unless so, unless we concentrate heaven in the person of Christ, and believe in His bodily appearing before God for us, then are we set to a harder task in our worship than were ever the ancient people of God. We need such an aid as is here given to keep the distinct personality of God before us. We are not to mingle Him with His creation, but are to pray to one who is separate from all He has made. So the Bible tells us of heaven, where His throne is set. Of the reality and position of this dwelling-place of God it is enough for us to know that Christ is there. Knowing this, God cannot be lost to us. Wherever man is, there is a heaven above him ; and from the spot he stands on, he may appeal to God through Him that is the Way. It is not to an idea of our own we appeal, but to a separate, definite person, who hears when we say, " Thou." We do not make His presence by falling on our knees; He was before we prayed, and was present before we realised His presence.

But the leading idea put into our minds by our Lord is, that as God will help us as our Father, so can He as being in heaven. As David says, "Our God is in the heavens, he hath done whatsoever he hath pleased." From the darkness of earth we pray to Him who is in the light of heaven; from the confusion of earth and its perplexity, we pray to Him who sits above, seeing to the end, and ordering all things; from the trouble and weakness of earth we cry up to the "blessed and only Potentate, God over all, blessed for evermore." It is good for us to remember that there even is a heaven as well as an earth; a place where God's rule is seen, and where all is harmonious, well-ordered, steady, peaceful, as the blue vault that symbolises it. But how much better to direct our prayer into that kingdom, to its centre and throne, and thus to fasten and secure our hopes in the world above, where there is no more curse, and where they dwell who even now have overcome. This is our comfort, that while we are involved in this world we can appeal to One who is above it. and uncontrolled by it. Or this might be our comfort, did we not bring God also down to earth, and either lose sight of Him amid its confusion, or bind Him helpless with His own laws. Our prayer will not proceed in faith until we raise God high above us and all that we know, to the very supreme of power. When the utmost skill and strength of the child have failed, he runs to his father, never doubting that with him is more skill and sufficient strength. And we must learn to cease from measuring the power of God by our own, and reasoning from the one to the other. We must learn to set God above His own laws; not that He will reverse them, but use them as we know not how. We are not to think that, where we see no possibility, God sees none; that, when all human skill has been fruitlessly spent, there is no more that God can do; that, when everything goes wrong with us, and we are ready to sit down and wait for ruin, there is no help for us in God. Too often we pray to a God whom we do not set in the heavens, to whom we do not in fact ascribe as much wisdom and power as we do to men, whose help we do not as fully trust in as we should in the combined help of some on earth we know of, whom we scarcely trust in much more than in ourselves, else we should not be found despairing when we see no remedy for our ills and when our own strength is exhausted.

Again, this invocation sets before us a God of heavenly holiness as well as of heavenly power. In the God to whom we pray centres all influence for good, and from Him proceeds no evil. Every exercise of His power has been, and continues to be, on the side of good. "He cannot be tempted." No circumstances can combine to make Him favour evil-doing or neglect well-doing. It is of His nature to help, to give, to bless to the utmost. Free from all suspicion, because He knows what is in us, He appreciates the feeblest beginnings of good, cherishes and fosters into life what man would count dead and lost, knows nothing of the grudging, of the malice, of the captiousness of man, but watches how He may encourage us in the slightest efforts towards the right, watches how He may insinuate His help, and in proportion to His own freedom from all taint or shadow of evil, deals delicately with the sinner in all His way, until our eyes begin to open to the perfect rectitude, simplicity, and loveliness of His character, and we see that in Him there is help for us in all good, and deliverance from all evil. And when we see something of the holiness of God, we shall be careful to restrain such desires as are inconsistent with His purposes, but shall very boldly expect that He will " hear the right."

It need scarcely be said, that the word " our," by which we are here taught to address God, can by no means prohibit or discountenance the individual and private use of this prayer. But our Lord, viewing the need of the whole body of His people, gives one prayer for all, and it is when we pray together and for the things we need in common with all men who have lived through this world, that we feel the certainty of our being heard grow to its height. We then but swell the common voice which has gone up to God in all times and from all corners of the world, which has passed to Him from the un-hardened lips of the child, and which He has caught up from the broken utterances of the dying ; which has been sighed as a forlorn hope by the despondent and oppressed, when all other hope seemed vain, and which is gradually risen to, through other prayers, as the highest and most hopeful utterance of Christian faith—an utterance which, like the highest flight of angels

on Jacob's ladder of prayer, carries the soul out
of sight of earth, and, giving it the vision of the
things of God, teaches it what is worthy to be
desired. Round this prayer the desires of all the
faithful cluster, and here we enjoy the communion of saints. Praying in remembrance of
that great company of our fellow-men in whom
we see more legibly and variously written all the
sorrows and anxieties, all the pains and sins,
that are incident to our common humanity, we
learn what are indeed our deep and urgent needs.
No more blinded by our own peculiar and immediately present circumstances, we learn to see
through them to the wants which lie at the
ground of our nature, and always exist. And
thus we are taught what to pray for, both by the
company in which we pray, and by the nature of
Him to whom we pray. Praying with our fellow-men, and excluding no most distant character, nor saddest condition, nor deepest necessity,
our hearts expand to desire those larger blessings
which embrace our whole beings, and do not
limit prayer to those particular benefits which
touch only what is peculiar in our present case.
And praying to the holy and loving God, our
hearts renounce evil and earthly desires, and rise

to things that are worthy to be given by the Father of glory.

The propriety and breadth of this invocation are thus readily appreciated. To use it rightly, with the understanding and the spirit, is to begin prayer as we ought; confidently and lovingly, because we pray to "Our Father;" humbly, because we call God "Father" only through the humiliation of the Son; hopefully, because all power is with Him; carefully, because He is holy. When we are drawing near to God, as if we were hardly used, as if our misery were giving us a claim, as it gives God occasion of mercy, then this "Our Father" reduces our spirits to a lowly and suitable thankfulness. I cannot be hardly dealt with if I can say to God, "My Father." When we are drawing near recklessly, more because the time of prayer has come round than because the heart is hungering after the things of God, does not this "Our Father" bring before our thoughts all the toil of Christ on our behalf, His incarnation and His passion, His ascension and His ceaseless appearing before God for us, and forbid us to use lightly what is so earnest a matter to Him? When we would gladly have the blessings of God's bounty and the security of His favour, but would rather have these at a distance from Himself, than come into any connexion with Him which would oblige us to lead a holy life, does not this "Our Father" profitably remind us, that relationship close, enduring, and assimilating, must be the beginning of all hope and blessing? When we are entering on an act of devotion, as if it were a mere exercise of the spirit, in which none is concerned but itself, this invocation reminds us that prayer is something more than "a posture of the soul," a beneficial state of mind, an under-going of certain trains of thought and emotion, that it is address to another, transaction with a personal, present, living God. In short, this introduction suits itself to every praying spirit, attracting and encouraging and filling with all suitable thoughts and feelings.

Let us, then, use this common prayer with intelligence, striving always to fill it more fully with meaning and desire. Let us wait for no other introduction than that which is given us here; and, seeing that it is no stranger who asks for our worship, let us believe that thus He would have us get over that great difficulty of drawing near to Him suitably, and let us ask from Him, than whom none is nearer, none more intelligent of our condition, none more considerate, none more painstaking about us. And as we have the faculty of love to attach us one to another, which makes solitude wearisome and friendlessness terrible, so we have this faculty of worship which is relieved and finds its object, when we return from our distance and banishment, and fall down before God, and say, " Our Father which art in heaven." This is love, and admiration, and trust, the most absolute. This is the ultimate repose of the spirit, beyond which nothing is desired, nor can be conceived. This is the feeling which at last says, " It is good for us to be here; here let us dwell, even in thee, O Lord, who art our dwelling-place in all generations."

II.

" Hallowed be thy Name."

OF the petitions which are included in this
prayer, none has been less prayed than this
which our Lord sets first.   Many a man has
cried earnestly and sincerely enough, " Give me
this day my daily bread ; " many with deeper
earnestness, and out of a more appalling helplessness, have cried, " Deliver us from evil ; " but
few have learnt to have this petition deepest in
the heart and readiest on the lip, " Hallowed be
thy name."   At all times we recognise it as very
proper, but rather as a doing of homage to Him
we invoke than as the first soaring petition, in
which the spirit, feeling its liberty and rejoicing
in the wealth of its prospect, rises at once to the
very summit of all desire.   Is there not this
feeling still in our hearts, (and is it not one that
must be got rid of,) that to desire God's glory,
and pray for it before we tell the wants which

are gnawing our spirits with very sensible agony, may be a seemly and decorous order, but is certainly not the natural one ; that, if it be right to seek the glory of God first, this must always be with us an artificial order ; that the habit of our minds is so constantly to make for our own good that it can only be by constraint and correction we can reverse this habit, and seek other things as heartily ?   Now, prayer demands that the very order of it be sincere, that we do not set first among our petitions what ranks among the last of our desires, nor think to propitiate God by an artificial introduction wrought up beyond our feeling.   The aid of the Spirit is afforded us that the deep-seated longing for the glory of God, which has seemed impossible to us, may become not only possible, but habitually predominant.

However, that we may not set before ourselves a higher attainment than God has set, and higher therefore than we can achieve, and so, instead of rising, sink into a despairing helplessness that gives up all effort, let us remember that God's glory and our own good are so connected that we cannot desire the one without also, at least indirectly, desiring the other ; as little as a soldier can eagerly advance the glory of his commander without thereby advancing himself. And as there are times when the only way to secure the good of the cause in which he serves is to give his whole thought to the providing for his personal safety, and when he is so tumultuously and pressingly surrounded with dangers, that it were idle to ask him to think of anything else, or desire definitely anything else than his own deliverance and victory, so there are times when a man's personal wants so throng before him, and when his own condition is so critical, that to ask him to pray for anything else than personal help and deliverance would be useless and wrong. For what so desirable as that a man be brought to God by the intense agonising desires of his own heart, and should own, out of his personal and unmistakable experience, that with God are blessings which must be had now, and before anything further can be thought of ? But this prayer, while by its individual petitions it satisfies these occasional moods, is specially adapted to our ordinary condition, and teaches that to an unperturbed mind, calmly surveying the desirable state of things, the glory of God will appear to be the comprehensive and prime blessing, which, if secured, all else will go well. We are to desire it not as

something different from, but as including our
own good; nor yet are we to desire it for this
one reason only, that it includes our own good,
but in view also of all that other good which is
besides embraced in it. The right condition of
things, the well-ordered and firmly-established
condition, in which we may eternally abide with
security, gladness, scope, and highest energy, is to
be attained by this prayer; surely, then, first of
all must God, the centre and head of all, get His
place in the world. Should we believe that this
was a prayer to be trusted to, did it open with
any other, any lower petition? Is not this at
least a good beginning, a sure foundation? Is
not this that which all men, at all times, may
agree to desire?

But though these words, " Hallowed be thy
name," are a distinct petition, and not a mere
appendix to the invocation, yet without the invocation we cannot understand nor use this first
petition. For to think of God as we naturally
do, and pray that His name may be hallowed, is
impossible. The names by which our untaught
hearts would call God are such as these, distant,
inexorable, unsympathising, grudging; inhabiting
quite another world than ours; separate from, and

even ignorant of, all influences which move us; having a will to humble and tyrannise over and baffle us. If such be the names which best represent our idea of God, then of course we cannot pray, " Hallowed be thy name." But such is not the God to whom we have been introduced by Christ; He has taught us to say " Our Father ;" He has come and, without upbraiding, has convinced us how totally we have misunderstood God. He has taken the veil from our hearts, and the fixed aspect of eternal and unalterable love moves us to humility and wondering devotion. He shows us how, while we have been forgetting God, He has been thinking upon us ; how, while our thoughts toward Him have been full of suspicion, and weariness, and aversion, His towards us have been " precious," fraught with ineffable compassion, forbearance such as the patience of God could alone exhibit, and a marvellous goodness which has taken up every feature of our necessity, and being still unexhausted by this great draught upon it, has liberally and rejoicingly showered upon us lavish and unthought-of blessings. He has shown us above all, that, while we have been seeking to sever ourselves from God, He has been connecting

3

Himself with us, so that no interests can be dearer to Him than ours'; that "hitherto hath the Father worked" and the Son for the unconscious and helpless younger brethren; and that His care being to provide for us, His purpose to prosper us, His glory our well-being, and His Son our elder brother, He would have us know Him by this name, "Our Father." And when we are moved by the Spirit of adoption to call God by this name, and to believe that there is one family in heaven and on earth, called by the name of the Son of man who came down from heaven ; when we look to the face of this Father and see in its loving wisdom and majesty and truth that verily He is also God ; when we survey the excellences which belong alone to Him whose love thus embraces us as in a sure dwelling-place, then glorying, we glory in God ; and saying, " Our Father which art in heaven," we say in the same breath, in the same burst of feeling, " Hallowed be thy name." We need not the old admonition, " If I be a Father, where is mine honour ?" For the time, at least, we have the feelings of God's children ; and what so dear to the heart of the child as the honour of his father's name ?   As we approach and address

Him our hearts fill and swell with a sense of His boundless might and marvellous counsel, of His supremacy in dominion and in excellence, so different from all else that He is seen to have right to His name, " I am, and there is none else beside me," and yet—" Our Father ;" so separated from all besides that He and they cannot be named under the same kind of existence, and yet " Our Father." How can we but long that all men should revere this name, and should come to such knowledge of it as to live by it ?

But what precisely are the feelings we express when we say, " Hallowed be thy name?" Is the name of God of similar use and meaning to the name of a man ? A man's name is that by which we speak of him to distinguish him from every one else. When we use the name of any one, it calls up to our minds a certain character, not always according to truth, but according to our idea of the man. And so, when we hear or use the name of God, there is also present to our minds a certain character ; too often a character made up of the ideas which we have thoughtlessly suffered to cluster round the name ; sometimes, however, a character which does on the whole agree with what God has taught us to believe about Him. The name of God is not God himself, neither is it our idea of God, but it is that expressed idea of Him which He himself would have us to possess, and which may be gathered from His own revelation. The name of God is not the nature of God, nor His relationship to us ; but if the conception which God would have us to cherish of Him can be summed up in one word, then that word is the name of God. When it is said, "Some trust in chariots, and some in horses, but we will remember the name of the Lord our God," the meaning is, that confidence could be best maintained by remembering what God had taught concerning Himself. When it is said, "They that know thy name will put their trust in thee," it is meant that whoever has that idea of God which He himself by His dealings and teaching has warranted, will trust in Him. These dealings and teaching are not themselves the name, but rather the utterance of the name. From all that God has done and said gather up the various features of His character, and express these, and in that expression you have the name. The name of God is that which we can contemplate and say, "God is that."

This name we are not left to find out for ourselves. From the first it has been the care of God "to spell out Himself to us, sometimes by one perfection, and sometimes by another." One feature after another of His character has been revealed, until at length all has been shown us in Him who is "the express image of His person." Hint upon hint was given of the loving purpose of God to man, until all was told in the Word who declared the Father. Nearer and nearer did heaven seem coming to earth, closer and closer did God involve His glory with human interests, till the Son came and showed us "the Father." Nothing now can be added to this name; in it all that God is to us is summed up, and all that He is in Himself is implied in it. He jealously guarded His former names, and called the attention of men to each addition to His name, that the glory of this final name might be understood and received. To Moses He says, "I appeared unto Abraham, unto Isaac, and unto Jacob by the name of God Almighty; but by my name Jehovah was I not known to them," intimating as distinctly as may be that now He is about to reveal something more of His character. When He gave this name, He was about to bring out of an idolatrous country, and plant in the midst of an idolatrous world, a people in whom the knowledge of the one God was to be maintained for all generations. And so He calls Himself now by a name distinguishing Him from all usurpant gods. He calls Himself Jehovah, the I Am, the living God, who alone has life in Himself, the eternal and unchangeable One, which is, and which was, and which is to come. So hallowed was this name by the Jews, that they would not pronounce it; nor do we wonder at their awe when we read their books, and see what God himself made of this name. There, at the end of warnings that are terrible to read, come these words as the seal, "I Jehovah;" He who would be of the same mind to all generations, whose threatenings could not be vain, but were the expression of an eternal decision, of judgment passed with all time present to His eternal, all-embracing vision. And at the end of promises reaching far into the future, and speaking of things far different from the then present, come again these words as the firm ground of all assurance, the signature of God, "I Jehovah." This name was the fountain of all authority, and the guarantee of all confidence: a name asserting for its owner, what no other name ever did, the exclusive proprietorship of life; a "glorious and

fearful name," which set itself above every name,
and inhabited a glory of its own. But this name
was then given not only to preserve those wno
hallowed it from the hallowing of any names
which were unworthy of worship, but to be a
constant comfort and near refuge to them in all
their wanderings. Jehovah is the eternal, the
only God, because He only hath life, but also the
only dwelling-place of His people, because He
only is unchangeable. They had to be taught, as
we have to be taught, that not in this place nor
in that, but in God is the true rest. And so,
while they were led from place to place, thev had
God dwelling among them by striking symboi,
and they had the name of the Eternal and Unchangeable, keeping them in mind that He who
led them changed not nor ever passed away.

But to this was to be added a further name.
To know God as a rest and a home, even this was
not enough. It might seem at first sight to be
enough to know Him as the "I AM," who has life,
independent of all origin, independent also of all
accidents and contingencies, who possesses the
only true existence, and without whom nothing
else can be; it might seem enough to know Him
as the "I AM," the eternally Present, with whom

is neither past nor future, whose name is " I AM,' because in Him is no revolution of years nor succession and lapse of times. If He " is " now all that He ever has been, all that He ever shall become ; if all time as well as all place is embraced in His existence ; if by the name He has given us of Himself He has taught our faculties to strive to annihilate time and its changes and rise to His eternity, to resist our sinkings and waverings of faith and our varying moods, and to live now in all the peace and joy of a life that we have in the Eternal ; if He has taught us thus that with Him there is and can be " neither variableness nor shadow of turning ;" if He has taught us also to be independent of place, and has shown to us Himself as the One that is still with us, in whom we live, and who still brings us to the place that yields us the life He intends ; if He does all this, is there more that He can do ? Over the virgin mother's babe He pronounces a name which so fills the heart that it excludes all others. " Behold, I send a messenger before thee, to keep thee in the way, and to bring thee into the place which I have prepared ; obey His voice, for my name is in Him." And the name that is in Him is " Our Father," no longer a name that needs to be interpreted by accompanying symbols, but a name that "is in" the living person of Jesus Christ, and that we read as often as we look to Him; no longer the dwelling-place merely, but the Father in whom we are secured of refuge and rest; no longer the Almighty to whom we may appeal with sure hope, but the Father who "Himself loveth us," and whose care it is to accomplish our blessedness; no longer a "fearful name," the utterance of which overwhelms us, and the comprehension of which is above us, but a name which every child of woman can understand, and whose very simplicity attracts and wins us by its condescending nearness to ourselves. But this name excludes all other names, only because it contains all that was in them. It comes "not to destroy, but to fulfil." It was this name that the hearts of God's people were unconsciously yearning after through all other names that were given, until the Son came forth, for whom all revelation of God's nature and relation to us was preparing, and in whom all revelation is summed up, the Word whom God "has magnified above all His name."

It is this name, then, which we are to hallow. The prayer runs thus, "Our Father, which art in heaven, Hallowed be thy name." And so it is

of all the petitions: each is introduced by an invocation to " Our Father." It is our Father we
ask to rule us, our Father we ask to forgive us,
our Father we ask to lead us. And it is, along
with this, to be noted that this is a name which,
though at first hearing it speaks only of relationship to us, tells also and fully of God's nature.
The relation it speaks of is one that comes of
His attributes. It is not accidental nor arbi-
trary, but is so truly the result and free expression of the nature of God, that through it we
can read all that it concerns us to know of that
nature. And this will be obvious to all who are
accustomed to find in the incarnation and cross
of Christ the most evident manifestation of God.
So that we learn to pray that this name may be
hallowed not only because it is our Father's
name, but because the name of God is "Our
Father; " that is, we see that the name of God
is to be hallowed not only because of His connexion with us, but in view also of all the worth
which this connexion reveals. Beginning, it
may be, with more of gratitude for God's grace
to us than of vision of His nature, and springing
always from this source of grateful love, this
petition yet leads us to all the depths and all the

heights of worship. God would have us, first of all, to worship Him not as the Ruler of all worlds, but as bound to this world; not as attending to all parts of an infinite universe, but as regarding us; not, in short, as the Head of all things that are, but mainly and in the first instance as " Our Father." He confines our view that we may see more distinctly; this name does not show any part of His nature nor any portion of His dealings with which we are not concerned, but it runs directly between us and Him, and as through a glass which by confining magnifies and renders distinct, so through this name we are separated from distracting views of God, and led straight to all that He means to kindle our worship.

Learning what God is, we ask that His name may be hallowed or held sacred, regarded by all as a true and holy thing that is at any cost to be maintained in esteem, and under all temptation still believed in. May the idea of God, which He would have us to possess, be held as the choice possession of our spirits, the treasure on which our hearts rest, and to which they ever return; may it be held separate from all contamination of our own thoughts about God; and may it never be obscured by any cloud of adversity tempting us to think that God has changed; never lost sight of by any careless devotion of our thoughts to other objects and names; never presumed upon nor polluted as countenancing folly or sin, but cherished still and guarded as "the holy and reverend name of the Lord." For this is what we all need, the abiding assurance of the reality of God in the excellences of His nature and the grace of His connexion with us. How heartily would this name of God in Christ have been welcomed by those who felt after God, if haply they might find Him; how would they have welcomed the utterance of God's name in the life of Christ, as giving to them at last the knowledge of what is eternally right and good, pure and holy; as giving them at last one whom they could eternally worship, from whom they could accept law and guidance, and in whom they could trust for all. And this is what we also must find; if there be One, and who He is, to whom we may ever look up, and whom we may love and worship; whose actings are not biassed by personal leanings, nor fashioned by the customs or ideas of others, but are true and righteous; One who "is light, and in whom is no darkness at all;" One in whom we may trust without fear, because He is absolutely good, His love breaking down at no point, interrupted by no suspicion or coldness, yet never leading us astray, nor doing for us what needs to be undone. This is what we need, to learn and not to invent the name of God; to see His character displayed in a perfect, living person, that we may no longer guess at His thoughts and ways from our own, nor worship our own best idea, but may worship one whom we can call by name; whose name is written for us, and has become familiar to us, by the actualities of life, and whose name embodies and represents to us all that is absolutely and eternally excellent. And who that worships at all has not found his need of a more fixed idea of God? Who has not learnt that, if he is to worship at all, or pray to some more real object than a Samaritan god, he needs this for his first petition, "Hallowed be thy name?" This morning I found it easy to worship; God seemed near and living, as a second Person with me; His Majesty so patent, that humility was natural, and levity impossible; His holiness and love so evident, that my soul was rapt from all other objects. I did worship, and I worshipped God;

but when the remembrance of the morning bids me this evening seek a renewal of the delight, how different and how hard a task do I set myself! What seemed so substantial and living, has become shadowy and ideal only. He who seemed so attractive, that I was prepared to forsake all and follow Him, has put on the taskmaster, or the cold, repulsive indifference of the ruler of other worlds. The name of God has not been hallowed by me; profane feet have trodden the shrine consecrated to it. The examples of men have pressed out of remembrance the unalterable holiness of God, and I have lived as if holiness were not expected of me. Eagerness to compete with the world at its own race, has hurried me beyond the voice of God, and the restraining sense of His presence has been supplanted by indifference and forgetfulness. Once having fallen, I have thought myself unworthy or made myself regardless of God's forgiveness and aid, and have fought my own battles wiping the name of my Father from my heart. I have let go the thought of what God is to me, and have too freely admitted other claims. And now the name that I have so often denied seems untrue in my lips.

And not less for life than for worship do we need that the name of God be hallowed; for by a man's thoughts of God is his whole character formed.* Let him think of a god who delights in blood, and he will delight in the same; let him worship a god imperfect in holiness, and his efforts after holy living will not be many nor severe; let him think of a god who is pleased with ceremonies, and he will become a formalist; let him think of a god who can be paid by service, and he will become a hypocrite; let him think of a hard master, reaping where he has not sown, and gathering where he strawed not, and he will shirk every duty he dare, and tremble through a life of slavery to a death of confusion and dismay. But let him know God as his Father in Christ, and every influence for good that can be brought to bear upon the human character is enjoyed by that man. This knowledge will be the little leaven leavening the whole mass; the new centre in the heart round which each regenerated principle within us will take its place. It is an influence all for good, unlike that of the

---

* "Upon our thoughts of God, it will depend, in one time or another, whether we rise higher or sink lower as societies and as individuals."—MAURICE.

character of man, which mingles harm with its healing. It is the character which from the first has sustained, and to the last will sustain, all good that is found in man. It is because God is what He is, that there has been any holiness on earth ; because He loveth righteousness, therefore has He created men capable of righteous deeds ; because He has been demanding perfect holiness, therefore have those who hallowed His name bitterly mourned over their shortcomings, and have still persevered and hoped, because He is their Father. By His name, by the real and holy and aiding personality which that name keeps within our ken, is the inevitable and stimulating idea of duty cherished within us. These words, " Remember thy Father in Christ," (which have taken the place of " Remember the Lord thy God,"*) when spoken amid the tumult of the soul, have been as the monarch's voice, and have been enough to calm and lay its wild rebellion, to curb its passionate desire, to turn again to its rightful object the attention and homage of the soul. Under the most adverse circumstances, the name of God has still done its work. Through this name God has found entrance to the most har-

---

* See Tholuck on " The Sermon on the Mount."

dened heart, and uttering it over the dead conscience that has long lain buried under manifold
iniquities, He has quickened it to life and wake-
ful activity; in hearts that have been a prey to
all doubt, and whose doubt has been fostered by
all impurity of life, this name has enshrined itself
and round it has gradually been formed again a
temple of the living God; and it has still been
calmly and lovingly answering the doleful ques-
tions of despairing souls, and to those who have
either wickedly or in their weakness cried, " What
is truth ?" and " Who will show us any good ?"
its response has ever been, " Our Father." Hopefully as the morning star has it risen on the be-
nighted and weary; with healing and joy, as the
Sun of Righteousness, has it ushered in the everlasting " day which the Lord hath made," and
from which all darkness is passed away, and in
which we see God as He is, and discover the
holiness and the hope there is for us in Him.
Scattering all false ideas of sin and duty, all false
rules of life that have grown with our growth, all
blind thoughts of God which keep us murmuring
and unbelieving, this name of God has come into
the soul and said, " Now our Lord Jesus Christ
himself, and God, even our Father, which hath

4

loved us, and hath given us everlasting consolation, and good hope through grace, comfort your
hearts, and stablish you in every good word and
work."

And what the name of God is for individuals
it is for communities. If for our own land, or
for other lands, we hope for better things than
the present, these better things will be brought
about, when the name of God is hallowed—when
His name is declared to all, and believed by all,
and kept jealously and sacredly by all; when it
shines out from the contempt and misunder-
standing which overlay it, and is recovered from
the suspicion which banishes it; when it rises
above all the representations and tones of man's
utterance of it, and appears in its own purity, as
if written by the finger of God in the heavens;
when it is acknowledged by all as the highest
name, and receives from each a regard which
nothing else commands; when, that is, men learn
to look simply and constantly, intelligently and
devoutly, to Jesus Christ as the "image of God,"
and will suffer no thought of God to find harbour
and influence within them, which is not expressed
in His person. When men own God, and own
Him as the Father of our Lord Jesus Christ, then

will there be saving health among all nations.
When men come to the knowledge of the only
true God and Jesus Christ whom He hath sent,
then shall they have eternal life. Need it be
said that there is nothing else that will reform
the world than this, no other head under which
all things can be reconciled, no other centre
round which all can gather in love? Let all men
have one common idea of God, and that the true
one; let each man be a true worshipper of the
true God; let each in the solemn and secret
chamber of his own soul, where none seeth but
our Father who seeth in secret, be owning his
responsibility to his God; let each man lie pros-
trate and broken-hearted before the love of God
in Christ; and is there not already "Glory to
God in the highest, and peace on earth?" How
different a world would be that little world with
which each of us has to do, and which gives us
samples of its sin and its misery, could we say of
every one we had to deal with, "I may trust that
man to the uttermost; I may banish every fear,
and all suspicion; I may expect great things of
him, tor I know that far deeper than any earthly
influence can penetrate lies written on his heart
the name of God, his Redeemer and Father; he

knows and acknowledges God, and therefore acknowledges every right claim, he is already bound by an obligation which no entreaty, no persuasion of mine, could make more binding."

Let each one, then, look on his own life, and on other lives, and see the blank which God's answers to this petition might have already filled and may yet fill. Let him consider the place which God claims for Himself; let him give heed to His Word, "Let not the wise man glory in his wisdom; neither let the mighty man glory in his might; et not the rich man glory in his riches; but let him that glorieth glory in this, that he understandeth and knoweth me, that I am the Lord which exercise loving-kindness, judgment, and righteousness in the earth." And let him pray "From me, then, O Lord, remove all ignorance of thee, and all unworthy thoughts of thee; keep far from me all that is forgetful, irreverent, profane; cast forth from my heart all that opposeth and exalteth itself above all the name of God or that is worshipped; cast forth from thy temple all that sitteth therein showing itself that it is God; all my rebellious distrust of thee do thou graciously turn into childlike attachment and confidence; 'my presumption of thy indifference into hope of thy mercy;' grant to me the spirit of wisdom and revelation in the knowledge of thee, that, whatever fails me, my trust in thee may still increase, and that I may serve thee in love and acceptance, and my body become a temple of thine. And these things not in myself only, but in all others perform, 'that men may know that thou whose name alone is Jehovah, art the Most High over all the earth;' 'that all nations whom thou hast made may come and worship before thee, O Lord, and may glorify thy name.'" And this he prays, who with the understanding and the spirit prays, "Our Father, which art in heaven, Hallowed be thy name."

III.

"Thy kingdom come."

WHEN we find an earthly and a heavenly thing called by the same name, we are very apt to think of the earthly as that which better fills and satisfies the name common to both. When God calls a spiritual thing or a heavenly arrangement by the name of something earthly and well known, we look upon this as merely a mode of illustration, possibly a happy, well-selected illustration, but nothing more. We still look on the earthly as the substantial reality to which the name belongs, and deem that there is far more in it than will be found in the other. We think that the heavenly is only somewhat like the other, but will fail in some point. Thus, when God speaks to us of His kingdom, we are too ready to view this as but a figure of speech, which may intimate that the government of God over us does in some points resemble the sway of a monarch over his subjects; whereas the truth is, that this kingdom is the only one which comes up to the idea of a kingdom, which falls short in nothing of what a kingdom should be. "The Lord is King, not borrowing this title from the kings of the earth, but having lent his own title to them; and not the name only, but having so ordered, that all true rule and government upon earth, with its righteous laws, its stable ordinances, its punishment and its grace, its majesty and its terror, should tell of him and of his kingdom which ruleth over all—so that 'kingdom of God' is not in fact a figurative expression, but most literal: it is rather the earthly kingdoms and the earthly kings that are figures and shadows of the true."* What king but one fulfils David's idea of a king, the idea which he seems to have lived to learn, and which, dying, he left as a

---

* Dean Trench, "Notes on the Parables," p. 14, where the connexion of the earthly with the heavenly is fully discussed The following lines of Coleridge are worth remembering in this connexion:—

> "For all that meets the bodily sense I deem
> Symbolical, one mighty alphabet
> For infant minds; and we in the low world
> Placed with our backs to bright reality,
> That we may learn with young unwounded ken
> The substance from its shadow."

legacy to his people, and surrounded with an emphatic accumulation of authority that strikingly declares its importance? "These be the last words of David. David the son of Jesse said, and the man who was raised up on high, the anointed of the God of Jacob, and the sweet Psalmist of Israel, said, The Spirit of the Lord spake by me, and his word was in my tongue. The God of Israel said, the Rock of Israel spake to me, He that ruleth over men must be just, ruling in the fear of God; and he shall be as the light of the morning when the sun riseth, even a morning without clouds, as the tender grass springing out of the earth by clear shining after rain."

Who is there that does not expect (more or less consciously) that some time there will be a better order of things than now we know of? Who is satisfied with this temporary state, in which evil seems so native, good so foreign? Or, if satisfied, is it not just because we are aware that it *is* only temporary, that it is to be got over, travelled through to some better beyond? Who can believe that God will never manifest to men, how He can govern, and show in actual history the perfection of His kingdom and the benign influence of His laws? Who believes that He will never let us know how right and how salutary a thing it is to obey Him only? Nay more, who does not at least sometimes feel that this kingdom ought to be now, that now we ought to be living under one Supreme, together owning Him, seeing that He is not king elect, heir to the crown, but eternal King? Those at least who acknowledge the name of God, and who believe that He is, and that He is what He has revealed Himself to be, heartily utter this petition: "Our Father, which art in heaven, Thy kingdom come."

That it may be intelligently and earnestly uttered, we need to see distinctly what it is. In common with all kingdoms, it is a community, an organised fellowship of men, the bond of whose fellowship is that they all obey the same living Head. It differs from all other kingdoms in this, that its King is the most high God. The subjects of it are all men who are willing to become its subjects, all who desire to obey the will of God, rather than any other. No men, therefore, (it need scarcely be said,) are subjects of this kingdom by birth. "Except a man be born *again*, he cannot enter the kingdom of

God." Natural or fleshly birth introduces us to
the privileges of nature and of flesh. Birth in
time and for time, which has in it the seed of
eternal death, introduces us to the advantages of
time, and among others to the external and temporary advantages of the kingdom of God. Spiritual birth gives us the internal and spiritual
advantages. Born of the Spirit of God, we are
introduced to the eternal and peculiar privileges
of this kingdom. For "the kingdom of God is
not meat and drink;" does not secure the mere
protection and help which the kingdoms of this
world make all their aim and effort, but it is
within us. It begins not at the outside, but
within; alters not our circumstances, but ourselves. And therefore we are introduced to it,
not by some accident of our position in this
world, but by our own voluntary surrender to a
Person, by yielding the allegiance of the whole
soul and nature to a King, whom we choose as
our King for evermore. This may well be called
a birth, then, if for no other reason than this,
that it alters the whole character. It is called a
birth because it is the beginning of a new life; a
life which meets with no death, nor needs any
third birth to carry the man to a yet higher con-

dition. It is called a second birth, because it breaks off the life which the first birth began. and swallows up the death to which it exposed us. It is a birth in which our own wills struggle to life, but only because such is the will of God. It could not be called a birth, if we were ourselves the sole or the first agents in the matter; but can only be called (without absurdity) a birth, because we thereby become through the generation of another something which we were not before. If we are to know it as a birth, then it should be quite unnecessary to reiterate that it is not of our own originating. We are born again, because "the seed of God" is quickening us. One might have supposed that it would have been readily believed that we cannot give birth to ourselves; and how a man can at once believe that the life to which the second birth introduces is a real, new, and eternal life, and that the person born into that life is his own begotten, is hard indeed to comprehend.*

It is of God's children, then, that His kingdom is composed. It is our Father's kingdom

* It may here be observed, that "the will of man" (John i. 13) refers to the will of man begetting, and not to the will of man begotten. The opposition, "but of God," becomes thus more clear and telling.

we desire the advent of. It is the renewed will
which gives us entrance to it. But while this
kingdom is established within, it makes itself
felt and visible without. Finding its subjects
in us, it makes its laws be obeyed in all our
doings. It takes possession of every department
of activity, of every region of actual life. These
external things, are they our doings? This society, is it made of us? Then, if the kingdom
of God be within us, it will find expression there.
As it is impossible for any great earthly dominion
to be solitary, uninfluential, but is appealed to,
and must interfere, is imitated and must mould
others; so it is impossible for this kingdom of
God to be side by side with other influences and
not reverse, increase, or some way operate on them.
As little is this possible as it is possible to carry
a light through a dark room and scatter no darkness, but confine the light to the flame. This is
the mode of the kingdom's increase, and the promise is that it will so increase. It will grow till
there is no room for any opposing dominion on
earth. It will express itself, and in this expression will be found so to excel the kingdoms of
this world, that it will make for itself a new
heavens and a new earth. " For the kingdom of

heaven is like unto leaven, which a woman took
and hid in three measures of meal, till the whole
was leavened." And these two features of the
kingdom cannot be separated, its spiritual, internal character, and its outward manifestation and
progress.

But the name by which it is spoken of in the
words just quoted may suggest to some the idea
that "heaven" must be waited for, that this
prayer may be answered. And no doubt the
kingdom to be revealed, when the King appears
in the glory of His own person, will surpass anything that can be otherwise attained. But the
name seems to be used not because the kingdom
has heaven for its ultimate destination and sphere,
but because it is of heavenly origin and character.
It is for this earth we seek a blessing, when we
pray, "Thy kingdom come." We know that this
kingdom ought to be now. We do not look to
the future to accomplish that which is eternally
right. We do not expect that death will transfer
us or others into a condition which Christ and His
Spirit can alone transfer us into. And being distinctly conscious that we ought always to have
been subjects of God, and grasping at the provision for our entrance into it, which is now put

within our reach, we do not wait, but pray and labour that all may be brought into this kingdom, that its laws may affect all earthly arrangements and earthly governments. This prayer in all its parts is emphatically from earth and for earth. And what we express in this petition is the desire that a heavenly state of things be established on earth, that the King and laws of heaven be acknowledged on earth. Is it not a right thing and a possible thing, that all men should in their hearts yield allegiance to God? And were this allegiance yielded, would it not naturally result that all our relations to one another would be hallowed and leavened by our common spirit of obedience? Would it not necessarily result that the whole constitution of the world, in all its domestic, social, and political arrangements, would be guided by the Spirit of God, and would show, if not uniformly and in every particular, yet generally, and, on the whole, that God was ruling? It is not required for this that all forms of government be changed, but that the spirit of those who administer be changed. It probably is not needful that many employments or relations of life be altered, but it is needful that we ourselves be altered.

The desirableness of this kingdom is obvious. The appearance of the King himself among us, and His manner of founding the kingdom, the blessings it yields to its subjects, and the final glory to which it is destined, all teach us to pray for its coming. When we look to its actual founding, it is not without significance that this was achieved at the most brilliant age of the most powerful earthly monarchy; a monarchy which may be viewed as the ultimate specimen of what earth can accomplish in the matter of government. For extent it was unrivalled. The world was the Roman world. For polity it was unrivalled, the system of its laws being yet received as the basis of law in the most civilised and well-ordered communities. It was when this empire was in all the flush and pride of youth that the King of God's anointing came and established His empire. He came with no noise and with little proclamation, no thunder of the captains and shouting. He came as if it were quite a simple matter to establish His kingdom, though the firmest earthly empire was in possession already, and though a firmer than all earthly monarchies possessed the hearts of those whom He came to rule. And how was this done? Most kingdoms have acquired

power by violence and wrong, this by righteousness and grace and mercy. To no other con-
queror can these words be addressed, " Gird thy
sword upon thy thigh, O Most Mighty, with thy
glory and thy majesty ; and in thy majesty ride
prosperously, because of truth and meekness and
righteousness." Sometimes the good done by
conquerors has well-nigh atoned for the evils of
war ; and their greatest glory has been to raise
the subdued, to overcome their barbarism, to conquer and to reduce them to civilisation. But the
glory of our King is, that He conquers us for no
other purpose than to raise us ; that He seeks us
not because the fame of our wealth and skill and
power had excited His envy or ambition, but
because the cry of the oppressed reached to
heaven, and the sighing of the prisoner came
before Him whose ear is delicate to catch the
feeblest and most distant, and to understand the
most confused desire of them that are in trouble;
who saw that there was none to govern us but
rulers who led us through tyranny to destruc-
tion ; He saw that there was no man, and won-
dered that there was none to come between us
and those who had us at their will, and therefore
His arm brought salvation. He saw that by His

government alone could we be rescued and raised, and he determined, through His own humiliation, to exalt us. He became one of us, that He might be our King; He clothed Himself in our dust, that we might wear His royal robe; He lay in our grave, that we might sit on His throne; He founded our joy in the deep bitterness of His own soul, our kingdom in His own obedience and subjection. Has He not claim to reign over us?

A government, once firmly established, goes on for the most part easily enough, sometimes quite independently of the throne; but it takes a man of kingly qualities to found a kingdom under the most adverse circumstances, and out of the most unlikely material. What was the case with this kingdom? This was no case of quiet, undisputed succession, nor was it one of easy and rapid conquest. Of men wildly rebelling against all righteous and conscience-binding authority, Christ took in hand to make a people so submissive that they may be called "living sacrifices." Of men who scorned His rule with a special scorn, He has to make subjects, who gladly lay down their lives for their King; of men hating one another, envying, maligning, and despising one another, He has to form a community so attached

5

that all possessions, and even life itself, are held as common property, and willingly yielded for the good of the whole; of men who, as soon as He leaves them, are invaded by His enemies, tempted, threatened, bribed, allured to disaffection, He undertakes to create faithful and stanch supporters; of those who are emphatically "not a people," He has to form a peculiar people, a people of God. And this He actually does. Men begin life wicked, selfish, profligate, with a strong revulsion of soul from all good, and a headlong proclivity to whatever is sinful, their spirits all in disorder, and seeking no higher condition; they acknowledge Christ as King, and His laws bring harmony and orderly purpose into their lives; in the strength of loyal love to Him, they make successful war upon their own fatal desires, and have often so well understood what is due to Him, that they have spent their substance and their lives in toilsome and bloody service. And does it say nothing for the reality, the force, and the wisdom of His government, that He can leave His newly reduced enemies to administer it, and Himself return to the seat of His dominion, sure that this distant province which He leaves will be a nursery of faithful servants, and ever send up to Him trained and efficient rulers? Does it not. at least, very sufficiently show that He is a King, though unseen; and that His kingdom is real, though not of this world?

Besides its origin, the difficulty and success of its establishment, there are many other features of it which evince its fitness to take precedence, and its worthiness to be desired. One of the most patent is its universality. It affords a meeting-place for all men, is capable of embracing all within it, and fusing them in one fellowship. Founders of kingdoms have not lacked ideas of universality. Their ambition has been very catholic. They have taken steps also towards the realising of their ideas; they have been careful to discover geographical centres, commercial centres, from which they might reach to all, and to which all, by natural leanings and interests, might incline; but so far as experiment has hitherto shown, it takes something more than worldly interest to bind the world together. By this, nations may work together for a while, but feeling that they are widely different, and that at any moment their interests may conflict. The bond is still without them, and not within. But in the kingdom which Christ has founded, there is a fellowship which does not recognise any distinction among nations. In it "there is neither Greek nor Jew, circumcision nor uncircumcision, barbarian, Scythian, bond nor free, because Christ is all, and in all." All own one King, all receive common rights, and all are actuated by the same spirit. In this kingdom we can claim nothing, as being of this nation or of that, but only as belonging to the one family in heaven and on earth. We stand upon a common ground with all, and enter a kingdom which excludes none. In it we learn the deepest affinity, and are drawn together by the only bond that is wide enough to encircle the world, and strong enough to draw together the unlikest. Whoever enter this kingdom resemble one another in the thoughts, feelings, and hopes that lie deepest within them, and which they count the most promising and permanent features of their character. Loyalty to their King possesses all alike, and this lies at the centre of the heart of each, working outwards and transforming all; and no difference, however great, can outweigh this resemblance, nor so increase as to obliterate and outlive it; for in this kingdom we are brought into communion with the " one Spirit, the one Lord, the one God and

Father of all, who is above all, and through all, and in you all." And here, too, is bridged over that wide distinction between dead and living, and are knit in closest bands with those who are advanced to the higher offices of trust, for "God is not a God of the dead, but of the living ; for all live unto him." Shall we not, then, pray that this kingdom come, obliterating all hostile distinctions, using all diversity of gifts for one common Lord, and putting one language and oath of allegiance in the mouths of all, " We are Christ's, and Christ is God's ?"

The advantages which the kingdoms of earth offer are commonly summed up in these three, Liberty, Security, and Plenty. A man outside of every community can assure himself of none of these. The simplest form of government is that in which a number of men choose one in whom they can trust, and who is expected to look after the common interests, while they attend to their special callings. There may be among them one so wise in counsel, so far-sighted, so large-hearted, so weighty, and so bold, that each member of the community feels "I am better in his keeping than in my own." And unless the subjects of a kingdom can thus trust the governing power for the leading advantages just named, it is not a kingdom to be desired. But we must beware how we compare the kingdom of God with earthly kingdoms, lest we thereby not merely see what blessings are to be expected in a kingdom, but learn to expect blessings of similar nature. A man may feel that he is safe as to many things, but what can he know of absolute trust till he has trusted in Christ? What can he know of any of the blessings of the subject till he becomes subject to Christ? Is not the liberty, the security, the plenty we know, very shadowy and precarious, until we possess the eternal reality and substance of these in Christ? Until we possess that security which has heard the gates of the city of God shut behind, and has found the feet standing on a rock; which can view every contingency without dread, knowing whose will it is that is done in the army of heaven and among the inhabitants of the earth; which can say, " Although the fig-tree shall not blossom, neither shall fruit be in the vines; the labour of the olive shall fail, and the fields shall yield no meat; the flock shall be cut off from the fold. and there shall be no herd in the stalls : yet I will rejoice in the Lord, I will joy in the God of

my salvation;" that security which is secure in
God, which rests in Him and knows that " greater
is He that is for us than all that can be against
us ;"—that liberty, wherewith the Son of God
makes free when He delivers us from our sins and
from all that drags us down from high apprehen-
sions of our calling in God; when He gives us
entrance into the wide and lasting love of God,
bringing us to the very brightness of His counte-
nance, to that love which casteth out fear, and to
that peace of God which passeth understanding;
when He renews the mind to the persuasion that
God is on our side against sin and all that comes
of sin, and enables us to accept of all that God
has been doing and does to free us from the
curse ;—that plenty which is supplied by the
fulness of the Godhead, and can only be enjoyed
in a kingdom where there are no unknown and
sunken masses, but where the King knows all
and rules by personal influence over each ; that
plenty which provides not for a few wants of
some, but for every want of all ; which provides
enlightenment of mind, renewal of heart, comfort,
strength, and every grace that is needed to bring
us to the measure of the stature of the perfect
man.

So that to become a citizen of this kingdom is just to reach the highest position a man can occupy, and to enter into everlasting blessedness. As among earthly kingdoms there are some so superior to others that it becomes a point of ambition to be enrolled as their citizens, because in them our rights are protected and our safety secured, because our labour receives its fullest recompense, and our liberty its freest exercise ; so there is this kingdom of God, founded from everlasting, and destined to endure when time shall be no longer, the which if we enter into, we shall at once be installed in a secure liberty, which is protected by the Almighty, cared for by that King, the meanest of whose subjects knows no grievance, certified of our eternal well-being, associated with all that is joyous and with all that is holy in the universe, and confirmed in every good resolve and rewarded for every good service by the favour of a loving King. This is the one kingdom which all others will be seen only to have pointed towards and taught us to hope for ; a kingdom so free that the law of it is love, so great that none are excluded and none unthought of, so righteous that murmur is never heard through all its borders, so stable that when neaven and earth are shaken this will "not be moved :" a kingdom so wisely administered that in it each one of us shall find his right place, when we shall learn the blessedness we have in common with all the nations of the saved, and that peculiar property of bliss, with which a stranger cannot intermeddle, and which is prepared for us by Him who has written our names among His subjects, and gives to us that new name which no man knoweth save Him that receiveth it ; a kingdom which we shall then only begin to learn the glory of, when we shall see it triumphant, and when the kings and nations of the earth do bring their glory and honour into it.

And this is the one perfect kingdom, because He who reigns is the perfect King, alone able to found a kingdom in the deepest love and broadest righteousness. He is King of kings and Lord of lords, He is the blessed and only Potentate ; but His special right of dominion over us is grounded in this, that He has taken our nature upon Him. It is as one of us, as *our* Head, as the Son given to us, that He takes the government upon His shoulder, and brings us to the kingdom of the Father. And do we need to pray that His kingdom may come, or do we not ? Are we sufficient for our own need, for our own future, or are we not ? Do we need some one to rule us, to help us against our enemies, to help us against ourselves, or do we not ? Have not our eyes opened to the fact that thick between us and God there stand those that bar the way, sins and hindrances of all kinds, that must be swept away or overcome ? Have we not tried to do this for ourselves, and found again and again that when the shout of victory was on our very lip, we were prostrated in the dust of shameful defeat ? Have we not felt at such times that all might yet be well with us, if some one, strong and mighty in righteousness, would only take possession of us, take us out of our own hands, and rule and command us by an authority more suasive than our own, and, imbuing us with a power that we have not of ourselves, make well-doing possible to us ; if some one would take up this cause which our feebleness is making nothing of, and would see to it, as for his own glory and as his own interest, that we be delivered, and conquer, and reach the peace of God ? What we daily find our need of is a ruler, and a ruler loving enough to give us all confidence in Him ; firm enough to support us when we weary, and

compel us to the right path when we waver,
powerful enough to do what man cannot do,
to change our hearts and deliver us from evil.
Such a ruler God offers to us, and such a ruler
we choose when we pray, " Thy kingdom come.'

The reasons why this petition should be used
with a special view to the extension of the Church,
and the encouragements there are so to use it,
are so fully before the thoughts of all praying
persons at the present time that less need be said
on these points. Of course the first ground of
hope that this petition is now to be answered,
more fully and visibly than hitherto, is just this,
that it is being prayed more earnestly and be-
lievingly now than hitherto. Prayer is not the
only means of bringing in the kingdom of God ;
but if it be, as we believe it now is, earnestly
prayed for, the other means will also be used.
And without prayer, earnest and sustained, what
can we look for ? Even the first descent of the
Spirit as the Spirit of the kingdom of Christ,
though certainly sufficiently provided for by the
ascension of our Lord, was vouchsafed only to
anxious and reiterated prayer. And in these
latter days there is no desire more common to all
Christians than that the Church may extend her

influence; nor are there any more conspicuous
features of modern Christianity than missionary
zeal. No doubt there is much in these desires
and efforts that is merely selfish and earthly, but
unquestionably there is also much that is of
heaven, and much too that is hopeful, because it
is not the unrooted product of a year or two, or
the mushroom growth of a passing excitement,
but the fruit of a steady growth which many a
year has nourished. This desire does not require
to be fostered by any special theory of prophetical
interpretation, nor can it in any time cease to be
among the most ardent desires of the Christian.
But no one can fail to draw some encouragement
from what he sees, nor can any one fail to see
that much of the progress around him is in directions which prepare a way for the kingdom of
God. Increased intelligence and a more general
and careful education, attention to the outcast,
the distressed, and the criminal, more liberal ideas
of civil liberty, the cordial, frequent, and increasing reference to union among different sections of
the Church, and many other features of the age
that are continually mentioned, all make our
prayer more hopeful. But while hope is our duty,
prophecy is beyond our province. Neither shall

we be much inclined to prophesy, when we consider these three things ;* how very different God's thoughts must be concerning His kingdom and the whole plan of its advance, from ours who see but the merest glimpses of His purpose ; when we think how often in past times there has been every prospect that now at last the Church would just steadily grow; and when we turn from speculation about the future to present fact, and think of "the millions afar off, that know not the Revelation of God, or of the thousands at hand that hold it in contempt." Yet these things only the more plainly show us that it is of God to grant that His kingdom may come.

Of the consummate glory of this kingdom it is very difficult to speak. We know that for earth the best condition would be the kingdom of God, but what earth will be when this prayer is fully answered, who would undertake to say ? It is ours to pray without ceasing, and to maintain fidelity to our King. We must cleave loyally to Him. He is coming in glory, and will reign whose right it is. Let us, if need be, endure hardness for a little that we may evermore reign with Him. No one can take from us His words,

---

* See Isaac Taylor's *Saturday Evening* throughout.

" He that overcometh will I grant to sit with me in my throne, as I also overcame, and am set down with my Father in his throne."

And for those who desire some detail of future glory to attract their hope no words can be more suitable than the following, written by one who spent his life in the service of his heavenly King, and has now enjoyed many lifetimes of reward. " O kingdom everlasting, kingdom enduring throughout all generations, where is never-failing light, and the peace of God, which passeth understanding; in which the souls of the saints securely rest, crowned with eternal gladness ; whither the ransomed of the Lord shall come, and everlasting joy upon their heads; they shall obtain joy and gladness, and sorrow and sighing shall flee away. O how glorious is the kingdom in which with thee, O Lord, all the saints shall reign, clothed in white raiment, and with crowns upon their heads. O kingdom of eternal blessedness, where thou, Lord, the hope of the saints and the diadem of their glory, art seen face to face, gladdening them every one, and embracing them on every side with the comforts of thy peace. There is joy unbounded, gladness unbroken, health untouched by woe, progress without pain, light without darkness, life without death, every good sifted from its ill, and enjoyed without alloy or interruption. Where youth never grows old and life never dies, where beauty never pales and love never cools, where health never languishes, where joy never wanes and where grief is never felt, where no moan nor sigh is heard nor any tear is seen, where gladness is ever enjoyed, and where there is no evil feared, because the highest good is possessed, which is to be always beholding the face of the Lord of rignteousness and strength."

IV.

"Thy will be done in earth, as it is in heaven."

IN the second petition of this prayer, we have prayed " for God's spiritual kingdom, that it may be set up and established in our hearts; for His visible kingdom, or Church, that it may increase and spread, until it fill the whole earth; and for His heavenly kingdom, that it may soon drive away and put an end to every kind of sin and sorrow, and leave nothing to be seen in the new heavens and the new earth but a glorious God, filling all things with His presence, and ruling with a Father's love over his dutiful and holy children."   Already, therefore, we have desired that those things be fulfilled which are contained in this third petition. We cannot desire that He be King over the earth, without desiring that His will be done on earth. We do not sincerely own Him as king, unless we set His will above our own and every other. For a kingdom where there is not one guiding will is a distracted kingdom, doomed to fall : a king whose will is not done is a mocked and virtually dethroned king. However, to add this petition is not to repeat, though it be to develop and follow out the preceding. The three petitions are to one another as root, stem, and fruit; as beginning, middle, and end. In the hallowing of God's name the foundation is laid for the establishment of His kingdom; it is the first opening of the human eye to the majesty of God. Then the kingdom is established, the heart of man prostrates itself before its King, forgetting and cancelling its old laws, and rejoicing in its new allegiance. But this is not all; no one praying would stop here. It is not enough that the kingdom be established, that its boundaries be enlarged, and its glory delighted in; there is an end for which all this is brought about; and that end is, that the will of the Ruler may be done. We desire that God may assert his dominion over us and all men, and may give us to know that He is a living and near God by the force of His will upon us. From the "name" we pass to the work (as displayed in His kingdom,) and from the work to the will.

6

From the outskirts of His personality we pass to its heart.

And we do not use this petition aright, till we fully apprehend that, besides names and outward show of authority, God has a will. This, of course, requires no proof nor theoretical explanation, but every one who is trying to pray knows how much need there is that it be practically enforced. How does his prayer seem to wander about searching for an ear, until the living will of God presents itself. When we think of God's name as left with us to make up for His absence, and keep us mindful of an authority which is resident in a person far distant from ourselves, we cannot pray. When we think of God's kingdom as established originally by Himself, but now left under viceroys or under a mere code of laws, we cannot pray. We need to meet behind the name a present will, and under all forms of authority and symbols of power to recognise an active will. From day to day, from one act of our wills to another, this we are to bear in mind, that God also has a will; that as by our wills we plan and set ourselves resolutely in one direction, so there are plans which have their origin in a will that is not of earth, but are yet to be carried

out on earth; that alongside of our desires there
are the things which God is desiring to be done.
Everywhere and in all things we are to meet this
will of God. This kingdom of God we speak of,
we have to learn to look upon as an absolute
monarchy, wherein one will is supreme, and beyond which is the outer darkness, where all is
confusion and dismay. And the peculiar discipline we have each of us to go through in this
life is to learn submission to the supreme will;
a hard and distasteful lesson, though so plainly
reasonable and necessary. Hard and distasteful,
for a man does not find within him a will piously
and wisely regulated by the will of God, but
diverging to his own evil desires, murmuring,
struggling, and only in the end, after long and
painful teaching, coming to desire that in all
things it be the will of God which is carried out.
It seems a strange thing that a lifetime should
be spent in this, and that the very highest employment of the will of man is to surrender willingly to God's will, but so it is. And when can
a man's will show its strength, if not when he
wills the same things as God? It is not that a
man gives up willing, nor resigns any property
of his being whatsoever, when his will is con-

formed to that of God; it is not that he becomes either the unwilling victim or the passive tool of another will, but that the whole strength and bent of his will now lead him in God's direction.

This yielding to the will of God, being a will so different from our own, is a great difficulty. We yield to-day, and to-morrow it seems as hard as ever. We gather together all the reasons there are for yielding, and at length we are able sincerely to pray " Thy will be done ;" we are very peaceful and very glad, and do not doubt that this is a final decision ; but an hour undeceives us, and shows us that the decision has to be made again, and in still more trying circumstances. If any petition needs to be daily repeated it is this. But have we ever once as yet thrown all the will we are masters of into this petition? Have we so much as recognised that it is the will of a person we ought all to be obeying here? Are we satisfied with some loose ideas of right and wrong? Do we go by custom, habit, fashion, impulse, our own wisdom, or are we led by this will? There is no question about this, whether God's will or my own has most claim to my service; which is getting most of it? Let me, if possible, see my true position; God has a will, a will about me as well as about other things; it is not, then, with mere rules of direction I have to do, but with an active and authoritative will; I will not hide from it, nor distribute its force over the whole face of the earth, but I come out personally face to face with God; will to will with God; and now what is it to be opposing this will? This is a will which has always been planning and accomplishing good—a will limitless in its embrace, and incom-- prehensible in its love—a will reaching to the most distant and stooping to the most forgotten and sunken, bending over distress, and raising the fallen with ineffable tenderness, and I cannot pray that this will may be done. This will, which has not ceased to "work for the deliver- ance and blessedness" of myself and all of us, which has still been that all men should be saved, in spite of untold hindrances and at infinite cost, this will it is that I have been resisting. This will into which no evil purpose ever entered, and the love of which man's heart fears to conceive, because it is above him, and seems unreal and im- possible; this supreme and marvellous will, of which it seems akin to profanity to say that it is

worthy to rule, I have scanned and misinter-
preted, and against it I have set up my own private desires, objecting to the plans of God, not
knowing my own nothingness before it, nor trembling before the great and loving Ruler in whom
it resides.

And unless we add to this the definite persuasion that this is an Almighty will, we shall
scarcely pray in hope for the performance of
God's will on earth. For we have done much
to engender quite an opposite persuasion by
neglecting and opposing the will of God. If,
however, there be not infinite power to execute
this will, then how is it to be done on earth?
What we see on earth is not readiness to accept
and execute it, but opposition, unflinching, full-
grown, consolidated wickedness; and if there be
not an Almighty will in opposition to this, where
is our hope? But He to whom we pray is not
a God that sleeps, or is on a journey, or talking,
engaged with and absorbed in other matters, but
a willing God, a God already attending, and
whose own purposes they are that we desire to
be fulfilled. The aid we have to expect is not
the very precarious aid we might receive from
dexterously availing ourselves of the power that

resides in the laws of God's kingdom; we do
not bring influences to bear on this earth which
may or may not reform it; it is the will of the
Almighty we appeal to. It is a new hope which
possesses us, when we come to the persuasion
that the will which we have opposed, and which
is yet our sole hope for ourselves and all men, is
powerful as it is loving. And it is a new resig-
nation which possesses us, when we see God, our
Father, the living, loving, ordaining Will, in the
midst of our lot, and can say, "Thy will, Thy
will—then it is altogether good. Thou hast been
the Author, Mover, Orderer throughout, Thou
hast planned and begun and watchfully carried
on, and therefore it is good. This Thou hast
done not by compulsion, but by Thy will, whose
will is done in heaven, whose will is leading me
to heaven."

Who shall say what may be thus contained in
this petition, or predict how, using it, we shall
be led from one degree of grace and blessing to
another, become more and more conformed to
the guiding will? Who shall penetrate the purposes of the only wise God, and tell the glory
which lies there in the seed, and which we shall
see with our eyes when God manifests what His

will is? And are we to fall out of this blessed track of His will, are we to be cast sadly ashore out of this river of life? Shall we be found dropping this petition from careless lips, as if the accomplishment of God's will had little to do with us or with the world we are in? Are we not already enjoying the fruits of that will? Am I not the child of this will? Is it not this which has made me myself and not another? "My substance was not hid from Thee, yet being un-perfect; and in Thy book all my members were written, which in continuance were fashioned, when as yet there was none of them. How pre-cious also are Thy thoughts unto me, O God; how great is the sum of them!"

But in our petition there seems to be an em-phasis on this, that the will of God is to be done. For as, when we have willed a thing, we do not sit down and expect to see it take place of itself, but set about the carrying out of our will by our work, so the will of God is not a thing to be spoken of, contemplated, waited for, but a thing to be done. And this will of God is to be done by us. For as a monarch does not rise from his throne to execute his own will, but has it exe-cuted by servants, to whom are allotted their several spheres of duty, so the will of God is given to us to do. It is still He who does it, but through our doings. The actual performance of His will has still been by the words and works of men. God has not been working in one place, man in another; but what God has done on earth, He has done by men on earth.

And here it is to be observed, that in order to our carrying out the mightiest schemes of God, it is not necessary that we know what these are. God gives to each what each can do, and by the various gifts and labours of all fulfils His own grand purpose. What we need to know is only the commands of God, what He sees fit for us to do. And doing this we may be sure that, so far as we are concerned, the secret purposes of God are being accomplished. He has given to all of us the same general orders, but by putting us in different situations, He does His will through each of us in different ways. One has little active work, but much to suffer. One is freed from the cares and temptations of eminence, but thinks his lowly condition not very suitable for doing the will of God. Another excuses himself from much reference to the will of God, because he is so distracted with the wills of men, and with their cares and burdens laid upon him. **All** such murmuring and excusing is vain, for these three things, God's commandment, our circumstances, and God's eternal purpose, are all of them springing from one source, the will of God, and do therefore harmonise. Our circumstances are allotted by the same will which commands **us.** And therefore let no one say, " I could do God's will better somewhere else." What is God's will you speak of? Is it not that you serve Him where you are ; is not that His will ? You were not made by God to be another man, and fill his place, and do his work. You were made as you are, to do your own work, and to fill the place in God's plan which He has appointed you. A weak monarch may mar his own design by employing his servants in posts for which they are most unfit But God does not so mistake ; He has " given to all according to their several ability," and so brings about His own ends.

So that when we pray "Thy will be done," we pray that God may so rule, that to the utmost ends of the earth, and in the minutest actions of men, and in all the arrangements of life, there may be the easily visible impress of God's will.

This we pray for, but more directly that our circumstances may be so ordered as to enable us to carry out most effectually the design of God with us, and that we may be so gifted with wisdom, courage, and self-command, as to see and follow out the line of conduct most appropriate to us where God has set us. Praying thus, we are strengthened for all duty, whether it be active or sorely passive. We find in all that happens to us an answer to this prayer, and instead of being dismayed, as those are who have not prayed that the will of God may be done, we find, in every change and seeming chance of life, new scope for carrying on the work of God, our share in His plan; and for our ordinary days, which pass as yesterday passed, we find no healthier influence to give them a uniform tone and character than to write on the threshold of each, "Thy will be done." I cannot come thus before God without some strengthening sense of the dignity and responsibility of a life connected with God, and fulfilling His will. I come to Him as my Father and my King, as if bringing my life in my hand, desiring that He would take it again, and give it back to me moulded to His design. I stand alone with Him, not confused by what other men are doing, not hidden from God's will regarding me by the practice of the world; I know that there must be something which God has for me to do, else I would not have life to do it; and can I go straightway and forget that it is not my own will and the world's work I have to do, but these only in so far as they are God's will and God's work? I cannot sincerely pray, "Thy will be done," and begin my day with no desire to know and execute God's commands; I am under orders, I have a purpose to live for, am no longer open to every influence that may blow upon me, nor can I any more count this life a mere vanity. And what higher purpose can a man have than this, to fulfil the will of God with him, and satisfy the reason of his being what he is, and where he is? Surrendering our wills thus to God's will, we live with a determined strength of will that nothing else imparts. We carry with us from God's presence God's authority, and in the strength of it we make the world serve God; we fulfil His will in the world and by the world, find this authority more suasive than the solicitations and examples of men; find in it a commission which turns this world into the material of God's work. If not, we have only mocked God in saying, "Thy will be done," mocked Him in a way which is most offensive to Him, calling Him "Lord, Lord!" but not doing the things which He has commanded; like the son of the parable, who said, "I go, sir," but did not the will of his father.

But very specially are we to dwell on the words "in earth," not suffering them to pass our lips without a degree of emphasis; for so hard is it to give ourselves, day by day, to the service of God, and to spend our whole time in the carrying out of His purposes, that we are tempted to give up this, and tempted by the most palpable delusions. And one of these delusions, which seems absurd when stated in words, but which nevertheless affects our conduct, is, that as in a future life we shall have opportunities of holiness such as we do not here enjoy, we are therefore not called upon to be living as carefully here as they do in heaven. Do we not find ourselves virtually saying, that because we have to live by our own exertions, therefore we cannot be doing God's will; that we must defer doing God's will till we get more time? Is there not visible in our conduct the want of duly remembering that on earth we must do God's will; to-day in all we have to do, for to-morrow we may not be on earth—the want of once for all coming to the persuasion, that what we are *here* for is to do God's will, not just to struggle through and reach death, but to live now as the servants of God; not to wait for holier times, but to redeem this time, *because* the days are evil; not to live as if we thought that hereafter we will be more bound to God as His subjects than now; and as if we thought that, though hereafter we may be expected to do His will, yet here we must do much that is not His will, much that is beside, and much that is contrary to His will, and that in the whole we cannot live with much reference to the will of God? Have we been praying with any true hope that God's will may be done on earth, or only believing that God's will may somewhat and sometimes modify the evil of earth, and may keep us from some of the grosser sins? Have we yet come to the strong sense of our responsibility, not to ourselves, not to our friends, not to the world, not to God's law, but to God himself; a sense which makes us say, "Here on earth I have something to accomplish, and that for God. This manner of life I am choosing, is this that which best accomplishes God's

will? If not, how do I pray, 'Thy will be done?'
In a thousand things I am choosing for myself,
choosing what I shall do to-day, what I shall do for
a time, whom I shall see, how I shall conduct myself towards this man and that; in all my choosing, am I referring to God's will, having resolved
to do it? Or am I snatching my short time
of wretched self-government, before God calls
me to account? Am I doing my best to shape
my life, so as to carry out God's will, or having
schemed a life for myself, am I wresting God's
will so as to bring it near to my own? Am I
acting from God's will as my reason, and motive,
and guide, or from my own untutored and unsub-
dued will? Knowing what the will of God is,
am I considering, Now how much of this can I
possibly achieve?"

And being so tempted to forget that through
all the employments, connexions, and circumstances of this earthly life, it is God's will which
must lead us, we must not cease, enlarging this
petition in words though not in meaning, to pray
and to desire "that we may be filled with the
knowledge of his will, in all wisdom and spiritual
understanding; that we may walk worthy of the
Lord unto all pleasing, being fruitful in every

good work, and increasing in the knowledge of God ; strengthened with all might, according to his glorious power, unto all patience and long-suffering with joyfulness." And if ever tempted to relax our efforts, if ever tempted to fall from the hope of this petition to the sluggishness which says, "It is impossible to do the will of God as it is done in heaven, and therefore it is useless to pray for this ;" let us remember that it is our sin that it is impossible ; that whether impossible or not, it is what we earnestly desire when in a right frame of spirit ; and that if it be so desirable, our part is not to give up because we cannot attain perfection, but to strive all the harder that we may come as near it as possible. It is one thing to attain perfection, another to desire it. And he who does not desire it here will certainly never attain it hereafter. So that the simple answer to the question, whether on earth we may pray for the perfection which obtains in heaven, and if it be not romantic or enthusiastic so to pray, is just this, that we pray for what we desire, and we cannot but desire to be perfectly serving God. It is vain to tell us we are too weak, too sinful, to reach perfection in this life ; this only incites us to put forth more earnest

desire and effort, and more beseechingly to implore the aid of "that glorious power which hath
delivered us from the power of darkness," "that
Almighty power which works (not indeed in the
doubting, but) in all who believe." That there
are things we cannot do is no reason why we
should not be doing all we can. And if no man
has reached perfection in this life, is there any
man who has done all he could to reach it?

But over against the sad truth that we have
omitted to make the most of this life, and are
therefore now not "perfect and complete in all
the will of God," over against the truth that there
are many parts of God's will which, on account
of our weakness, we have been unable to perform
as they in heaven do, let this other truth be set,
that there are parts of God's will which can only
be performed on earth. And would that we could
so understand this as to awake to the value of
this day we pray in, and bestir ourselves, and
throw our whole energies into this present life,
living out its duties with our might, exerting ourselves so as to arouse efforts which will lift us
out of our easy, natural level and rate of living,
and which will show that we have now one thing
to do, and one purpose to fulfil. To do the things

7

God's will now contains is not easy. We could not expect it to be so. Often has it been seen that, even among men, one dominant will has aroused thousands to hard, fatiguing activity, which, through the whole course of it, seemed all but beyond human strength; and shall we expect God's will to be easy and natural to us? And this difficulty appears very specially in what God has set before us all as our common aim and work, as the one thing He would have all of us to do, so that He says of it, "This is the work of God." This work is to believe on Him whom He hath sent. This we cannot do hereafter; it is the work of this life, the will of God for earth. This is that which will bring the best good to us, and the highest glory to God out of the apparent poverty and woe and vanity of this life. Is there any use we can make of our lives so profitable that, for the sake of it, we may neglect the saving of our souls? And if not, what are we to do? are we to sit still, to let ourselves be drifted we know not whither, when God has a definite will concerning us, and has given us a definite work to accomplish? But this work, easy though it seems, is found to be hard; it takes us to go out

of our way, to resist our inclinations, to pray as
our life depends on it, "Thy will be done."

Yet while the things to be done are different,
the manner of our doing them is to be similar to
the heavenly. We, the younger brethren, are to
look upon our elders as they do the will of God
in those higher posts to which we may not yet
be advanced. Letting our hearts dwell on the
blessedness of those who serve God and see His
face, we are insensibly assimilated to their spirit,
and are prepared to become rulers over greater
trusts than are here committed to us. And since
we cannot actually contemplate, and so imitate
heavenly service, this petition becomes a prayer
for the spirit of that service. We know that if
we be animated by the same spirit, the manner
of our working will resemble that of the heavenly
places. When, therefore, we pray, "Thy will be
done in earth as it is in heaven,"* we desire that
God's will be done on earth readily and cheer-
fully, humbly and zealously, faithfully and con-

* And surely it may be inferred from these words, "as it
is in heaven," that we are not to pray for the execution of
God's will in judgment, for this is not "as it is in heaven;"
not in opposition to and overturning the will of man, but as
converting the will of man, and operating through it.

stantly. And in looking to heaven as the model of our service, we need not pass by the visible heavens, from which David so constantly drew lessons for himself. To see how God's will should be done, we have but to turn the eye to the "unworn sky," old in the service of God, but fulfilling His will as at first. We see the precise regularity which should characterise our service also. We see how unweariedly all perform their parts, the great sustaining the small, the small reflecting and enhancing the glory of the great; all as members of one system, obeying in peaceful harmony Him who calls them all by their names. We see how the sun, morning after morning, comes forth rejoicing to run his race; how the moon observes her appointed seasons, and the sun knoweth his going down; how all, though it be in an unvarying course, fulfil the will of God untiringly. And is our glory to be our shame? Is the only result of our being gifted with will and intelligence, to be that we rebel against God, and revolt from His will? Ought not the order of nature, which we admire, and to which we trust, to be a continual rebuke to us?

But it is to the inhabitants of heaven we

are mainly to look, those "angels who excel in strength, who do His commandments, hearkening unto the voice of His word." "Hearkening unto the voice of His word," for it is this which makes them worthy of imitation, that all they do is done with direct reference to the will of God; because it is God's will, and not, in the first place, because they have chosen it. The throne of God is in their midst. They serve Him seeing His face, and what they see written there they haste to execute. And when our Lord asks us to pray this petition, He does not ask us to do what He has not done Himself. When He was on earth it was earth that taught heaven how the will of God should be done. Angels stooped to learn new devotion to Him whom they had already served without blame. And in the crisis of His life, the crisis also of the world's history, this was His petition, "Thy will be done." And so also we are to pray, Order our circumstances so that we shall have best scope for serving Thee, and reconcile us to our circumstances, and fit us for them, so that with our will and heart we may serve Thee. Preserve us from being conformed to this world; but transform us by the renewing of our minds

that we may prove what is that good and accept-
able and perfect will of God. Christ does not
bid us pray that this good thing and that may
be ours, but that God's will may be done ; for
this is at the back of all good, and embraces now
all the good that will ever be to any.

V.

" Give us this day our daily bread."

WHEN we set ourselves to fathom the character
of a man, we do not so intently observe the expression of his thoughts, as their connexion ; we
do not stand outside and listen just to what he
pleases to tell us, but, if possible, enter within and
observe the workings of his inner man ; we do
not care so much to know his ideas and senti-
ments in detail as to trace the links between them ;
so as to see the man, not only when he pleases to
emerge to the surface, but in the entire current of
his feelings and thoughts.   And, when we ascer-
tain those minor connexions of his various utterances, and can trace all that appears back to that
involuntary spring in the heart which suggested
it, we have a pretty accurate idea, not of what the
man desires us to think him, or even supposes
himself to be, but of his real character.   Now,
when we submit these two petitions, " Thy will be

done on earth," and " Give us this day our daily bread," to this species of scrutiny, we at once detect the character of their Author.   We see that He only could have thus passed from one to the other, who found it His meat and drink to do the will of his Father.   Many would pray, " Thy will be done," and many would pray, " Give us bread," but to how many of us would this have suggested itself as the natural order of these petitions ?

Are there not few who have chosen the trade or business they follow, because they thought that therein they could best work out God's will with them, compared to those who have made their choice as being the most pleasant, or most rapid, or most secure way of earning their bread : few to whom the supports and comforts of this life are practically of less importance than the doing of God's will ?   If we divide men into two classes, those who work because they are hungry and have to work, and those who work because there is something to be done; those who consider how they may best win a livelihood, and trust that in it they shall somehow find opportunity of doing God's will ; and those who make it their first consideration how they may best serve God, and trust that in doing so bread shall be given them ; we

need not say which will be the larger class, and
as little need we say which will be the more
Christlike class. It is in truth a very advanced
and enviable condition for a man to be in, when
he desires to be supported in this life mainly for
the purpose of doing God service. Yet not so
advanced by any means that none attain to it, nor
that we should be content only to envy without
striving to imitate those who have attained it.
How many reasons urge all of us to pray for continuance in life, besides this simple one which led
to the prayer of our Lord! When the mist that
has long lain gloomily on our earthly future
begins to lift and scatter, and reveals a fair and
attractive prospect; when plans are entered into,
the full execution of which will take years to
accomplish; when we have found a useful and
not unpleasant way of employing our time; when
we are surrounded with friends whose counsel
guides, and whose affection cheers and rewards
our labour, we have evident reason to pray, " Give
us still this day our daily bread." But therefore
ought we the more carefully to consider, whether
there be one reason stronger than all these,
whether there be one desire which at once and
uniformly suggests this petition, and would dic-

tate it still, though the world were blank of comfort and reward, and though natural feeling were
prompting us rather to say, " I would not live
alway." Not, of course, that we should be afraid
of cherishing subordinate reasons for continuance
in life, but that we should beware lest they become something more than subordinate, lest they
oppose instead of aiding the performance of the
main purpose ; not that we should be afraid of the
enjoyments and attachments of life, but that we
should always give the doing of the will of God
so prominent a place in our intentions and desires,
that we shall very naturally pray, " Thy will be
done on earth," and, therefore, in order that thy
will may be done, for this end and reason mainly,
"Give us this day our daily bread."

This petition, then, at once shows itself to be
quite of a piece with the whole prayer before us.
A petition for temporal support, it is a spiritual
petition. It presents the world as the godly
man sees it. Our meat and drink and raiment
first come into view here, and here we see them
from the heavenly side. This petition brings our
whole earthly condition before God, and readjusts
it before Him and with His help. It brings it back
every morning to its true position, from which it

veers and slides away in the forgetfulness and
pressure of the day's employment. Instead, therefore, of being easy, this petition is one of the most
difficult to pray. It is the petition that least of
all can be prayed from an earthly mind, for it
comes from the directly opposite quarter to all
earthly desires, and meets them on that very
ground to which they most tenaciously hold. This
is the petition of those who seek first the kingdom
of God and His righteousness, who "buy as though
they possessed not, and use the world as not
abusing it." Yet let us not fear to utter it,
though we know there is much that is selfish and
earthly in the desire as we embrace it, for God is
very ready to forgive the evil that is in our asking,
that so we may receive His gift, and with His gift
His blessing, which will purify us, and form our
hearts to heavenly aspirations through the knowledge of His love.

Here, first, in this prayer, we come upon this
word "Give," the key to the treasury of God's
riches ; a word that opens over us the windows
of heaven, that wakes the omnipotence of God,
and causes the fulness of His resources to flow
forth ; a word which is as a rod of power in a
man's hand, if he knows to direct it to the great

Giver, to Him from whom all things have come, who has given all out of Himself, and who continues to give not grudgingly, nor of necessity, but freely and liberally, because it is of His nature so to do ; a word that we must use, because we are poor, but which is put into our mouths because we are intended to be rich ; a word which, however often and greedily we use it, will still find its echoing "receive" in God. And there is no period when this word must be uttered for the last time, for God does not tire of giving, nor, like man, excuse Himself from giving more because already He has given so much, but by the further and more bountiful outpouring of His gifts satisfies that confidence in Him which His former gifts have inspired. And here this word "Give" stands in its simplicity, without apology, without circumlocution ; in its childlike boldness and straightforwardness of request. It is the wide opening of the mouths of the young birds hungering round the parent.

And it is remarkable, that the only introduction of this word in the prayer is when we ask for that which, of all things, we are most inclined to think may be got by our own exertions. We allow that there are spiritual gifts, which it is of

God to give. Or at least there are graces which we are aware we cannot have without God's aid, and which we feel so helpless to procure apart from Him, that it seems appropriate enough to call them "gifts." But here we are taught to depend on the simple gift of God, not for the wellbeing of our spirits, but for the maintenance of our bodies. We are to say "Give" of that which our whole time is spent in procuring. We are not to say "Provide," not "Put us in the way of acquiring;" but, however it is to be done, we are to say simply "Give," as if direct out of Thine hand into ours. What is true of the beasts of the field is equally, and almost as obviously, true of ourselves: "These wait all upon thee, that thou mayest give them their meat in due season. That thou givest them, they gather; thou openest thine hand, they are filled with food." Let society refine and involve itself as it will, let it secure itself against all contingencies, and provide regular labour and suitable returns for labour, still it is God whose is our life and breath and all things. This security and plenty, which make us feel less dependent on God than the savage is, who has to-day to find to-day's food, are only the more liberal opening of God's hand to us, showing us that we, if we are not more dependent, have more dependence on God than most. And the nearer we come to the actual procuring of food, the more evidently do we see God. We may stay at our work, engrossed by it; we may sit in our rooms, chambers, or counting-houses, and plan, and there we may see no one but ourselves providing our maintenance, and may fail to discern any symptoms of God's work; but when it comes to the end of all this, to the eating for life, we meet God and feel how utterly we are in the power of some other than ourselves. It is not we who make the corn grow, nor by all the appliances of science could extort one harvest from an unwilling earth. Must not the proudest and best skilled among us, after doing his utmost, just simply wait on God for His bread? This lesson, which one year's famine so feelingly and unmistakably teaches, seems an easy lesson to learn from the regular and ordinary supply which God maintains by sending seed-time and harvest in the seasons of His appointment. When we consider the vast number of lives to be maintained, the variety of food by which they are maintained in all different parts af the earth, the numberless contingencies, things that might so easily happen, but which, if happening, would hasten multitudes to the grave, the remote and various causes which must all of them be together regulated and ordered to this one end of life, are we not convinced that God is no idle spectator of the earth He has framed for man?

One thing more very strikingly leads us to acknowledge that we are bound to God as the giver of our daily bread; and a thing it is, apparently, intended for this very end. We cannot make food, do what we will; and as little can we store it up for years and centuries. Some things are given us in perpetual retention, once for all, and not year by year; thus we possess the stone with which we build, the coal we burn, and others of the most useful commodities. But the actual food does not so exist, does not exist dead and stored up, so that we can never run out of it. It is of earth's annual production, and has its term of life, after which it is useless to us. It differs from those things that the earth already contains, and which have only to be taken and fashioned by us for our use, inasmuch as it has to be called into being. That which shall sustain us in the years to come has now actually no existence. It must itself be born and grow, must itself receive life, before it can communicate life to us. And thus are we very plainly unprovided for, except in the faithfulness of God. The future is a blank to us except in so far as God fills it with His goodness. And in what a light does this set the character of him who eats his daily bread, not only as if it must infallibly and of some natural necessity yield him life, but as if he had made it and given it the life which now it gives to him! "Talk no more, therefore, so exceedingly proudly, let not arrogancy come out of your mouth, for the Lord killeth and maketh alive ; he bringeth down to the grave, and bringeth up. The Lord maketh poor and maketh rich ; he bringeth low and lifteth up." What we have by inheritance, and what we have by our own endeavour ; the abundance at hand, and the store laid up ; all is the gift of God, and through all our possessions we must pray to Him who is at the back of them all, to the Fountain of Life from which they are drawing all that can give us life. For this prayer is not a fanciful connecting of earth with heaven, an elegant way of making our life of drudgery for bread a life sublime, nor a foolish, meaningless homage to God, but it is an asking for what we need and can only have from God.

But there is another word in this petition, which we must take in connexion with this word " Give." And it seems, at first sight, strange that we should say, not only " Give us bread," but " our bread." The first truth which this suggests, when we pray, is, that what we ask for must be ours and not another's. We must, that is, ask for what God may give us without detriment to others. We are not to expect to reap what others have anxiously sown, nor to enter into other men's labours. " If any will not work, neither shall he eat." The bread we pray for is to be a gift so far as God is concerned, but it is to be ours so far as our fellow-men are concerned. We are to be careful that, in asking God to prosper us, we are not thinking of some other person's prosperity, and wishing that some of it were transferred to our lot. We are not to push our own interests regardless of the interests of others ; still less, so as directly to injure others. We are to keep within our own domain and the limits of a fair and open competition. This prayer, then, saves from dishonesty and cruelty. When we thus pray, we see that our advancement is to run in the line of God's pleasure ; and we are enabled to choose rather to wait to see His

8

way of prospering us brought to pass, than to take the matter into our own hands, and, by means pleasing to Him or not, to make a competency for ourselves. It is bread provided honestly in the sight of man that we are to look for, and not the bread of idleness, of deceit, or of extortion. And, therefore, when we say, " Give us our bread," we do not expect that God will lift us above the common and toiling ways of men, nor loosen us from the hard and burdensome conditions of this life, raining on us bread from heaven; but we trust that He will find for us labour, such as shall not only win us bread, but be otherwise beneficial to us.* And thus God, in that word of His which Christ rested on in the time of His trial, says, " Man liveth not by bread alone, but by every word that proceedeth out of the mouth of God "—that is, not by the simple and visible gift of God, but by His disposition of our circumstances, and distribution of natural ability to labour, and scope for exercising this ability.

But, again, this word " our " teaches us to be considerate in our desires, and discriminating; to ask not blindly for the good things we see

* Stier quotes a striking proverbial saying, " We lift our empty hands to heaven, and God lays work upon them."

others enjoy, nor for all that for a moment strikes us as desirable, but for " our " bread, for that which is suited to us in our present position. What others are receiving, and may be both delighting in and profiting by, might be a very disastrous gift to us. This is, then, in other words, the wise prayer of Agur, " Feed me with food *convenient for me.*" And while there are hardships in poverty, which none will make light of who knows anything of their variety and their bitterness, yet, if this be the condition appointed to any, let these also thankfully pray for their pittance from God, remembering that He who taught us this prayer Himself lived from day to day, not knowing in the morning where the evening meal was to come from, not knowing in the evening where He would find shelter for the night, having while alive no home He called His own, nor when dead a place provided to lay His body, possessing nothing while in the world, and leaving behind Him no more than the raiment He wore. Though this be a condition which we cannot desire, yet it has its own blessing, and those who find this allotted to them as their daily bread, will (if they are receiving it thankfu'ly from God) find in the end that no better condition could have been assigned them, and that it has been no small inheritance to share the poverty of their Lord.

Again, it is perhaps not straining this word to find in it a reference to, and prayer for, others along with ourselves. In any case such prayer is very suitable, but it is specially appropriate when we pray for the provision of this life : inasmuch as in this we are all dependent one upon another, no one man's work sufficing for the actual accomplishment of his own sustenance, clothing, and comforts. In the savage state, men may be excused for some selfishness, where they can live in all things independently of one another, each man building for himself and catering for his own wants. But we are inexcusable, if we be not charitable, not only in prayer and intention, but in deed, we who daily enjoy what has cost the labour of many. And the more we live in liberal community with others, the better will our lives appear in the end to have been spent.

On the whole, then, this word "our" teaches us to desire to be laborious, contented, and charitable ; to work with our will and strength, doing our best in our place ; to wait on God for fruit of our work and returns for our labour ; and, receiving these, to be satisfied, if they be small, and willing that others should share with us, if they be large. He who has to earn his bread is girt by this prayer with a fresh and cheerful confidence for his daily duty : and he who has abundance is admonished to be diligent in the right disposal or increase of it, knowing, at least, that this prayer has not been from his true desire, if he leaves to their hunger and misery any whom his further labour might relieve. For our cause is a common cause with all mankind, as our Lord's self-sacrificing life stands ever teaching us ; and while there is want in the world unsupplied, there should be no faculty of labour in the world unexercised. If the healthy do not work, what is to become of the sick ? If the strong man do not labour, what help is there for the child and the aged ? And to those who are labouring to their utmost, and yet not seeing the results they purposed and still desire, all that can be said is, Wait and pray this prayer still. This is all that can be said, not because your case is a desperate one, but because in this all consolation is included, and all hope, as you well know already, if the Spirit has taught you to say in simplicity, " Give me this day my daily bread."

By teaching us to ask for bread, our Lord indicates that our desires for worldly good should not be passionate, but moderate; restricted to the supply of the natural wants of our condition. For this the word *bread* naturally suggests to us. We say that we do not desire a great deal, but enough to enable us to do God's will effectively, to be the most we can.* It is not a burden of luxuries and superfluous comforts, but the light equipment of a hardy abstemiousness, which is aimed at by this petition. We acknowledge the propriety of leaning rather to what is severe than to what is sumptuous; and while we by no means deprecate all extras, all comforts and pleasures, these are not sought with the fervency of prayer.

Here, accordingly, the question emerges: Can a man conscientiously pray thus, and straightway proceed to his employment, resolving to acquire, if possible, far more than enough for the maintenance of life? The answer to this has been anticipated, when it was said, that the honest offering of this petition impels a man to labour

---

* Clement of Alexandria cleverly compares a man's possessions to a shoe. They must fit him; being cumbersome and uncomfortable if too large, as well as painful if pinched.

to his utmost. Let him make what money he can, if that be fairly in the way of his calling, only let him, more than any other, keep repeating to himself the reiterated warnings of God's Word concerning the entangling power of wealth. Let him start right from the petition preceding this. Let him be sure that his chief end in seeking gain be to do God's will on earth. Let him be very certain that his purpose is to employ his gains in a manner on which he can ask God's blessing; and let him through his whole career examine himself, to learn whether the means be not becoming more to him than the end, whether his desires are still going beyond the gold to the Christian expenditure he at first proposed. No doubt this requires a strong and watchful spirit: but since commercial ability, as well as every other talent, is to be consecrated to God, and since money is needed on all hands for the best of purposes, let him who has the ability to gain use this petition, and what he receives as God's gift he will use in His service. For do we not all feel, when we use this petition, that we must not use what God may this day give us, for the pampering of appetite, for the vanity of display, for waste, for anything which will not please

God? We know how it has grieved ourselves to see what has been besought at our hands put to a use which the receiver knows we abhor or disapprove, and we determine to show ourselves worthy stewards of the gift of God to us, and to justify (so far as in us lies) our appointment to so many blessings.

And as our prayers are moderate, so let us be thankful for ordinary benefits. For wherever there is material for prayer, there is material for thanksgiving. If we need to pray to God even for our bread, then even for our bread let us give thanks to Him. If to-day's supply does not come by chance, nor because we were similarly supplied yesterday and the day before, but because God regards our wants of to-day, and for this day also grants us life; then this day ought we to thank Him for this day's mercies, though they be but the same as yesterday's, and what all other men are enjoying. As each rising sun, touching the wing of the sleeping birds, wakes through the woods a fresh burst of glad melody, as if sun had never risen before;* so let each day's mercies awake our hearts afresh to the sense of God our Father's smile, and turn our lives towards His

* See " Three Wakings," and other poems.

light. "Where nothing is deserved, everything should be received with thanksgiving;" how then shall we ever discharge our debt of thanks, who deserve to know the power of God's anger, but experience the power of His mercy?

There is another essential of this petition. We are to pray for this day only. And this is a point of so much importance to the right ordering of the godly life on earth, that our Lord follows it out in the subsequent discourse, and impresses it with a beauty and force of persuasion which have made this a marked passage of Scripture. He anticipated the objection that we must provide for to-morrow as well as to-day, and reminds us that He who clothes the lilies of the field, and makes provision for the birds of the air, knows that we also have lives to be maintained, and constantly recurring necessities. By reminding us of our helplessness, of the folly of distracting forethought, and of the sufficiency of the care of God, he shames us into confidence. "Is not the body more than meat?" He who has given you the greater, will He not also provide the less? "Is not the life more than raiment?" He who can create and maintain the one, may well be trusted to supply the infinitely less costly want. "Are ye not of more value than many sparrows?" And yet is one want of one of these overlooked, forgotten, or despised? Does God find pleasure in lavishing on a flower which the eye of man never sees, a beauty which no forethought or effort of yours could produce, and will He spend no care on you, O ye of little faith? Does He not know what you have need of, so that you are constrained to be fearful and anxious in your own behalf? Or can you really, by all your pondering, provide one crumb beyond what He has provided for you? Does your scheming by day and by night remove you out of the care of God into an independent and self-supporting life of your own? "Take, therefore, no thought for the morrow, for the morrow shall take thought for the things of itself. Sufficient unto the day is the evil thereof." Bring not, then, into this day's cares, and to confuse the duties which this day requires of you, to-morrow's cares and anxieties about its duties. I here ask God to take me through this day; if to-morrow comes, He knows that I shall be as dependent on Him then as now. But it forms no part of my care; I have cast it on Him.

But does this forbid planning of all kinds? Does this preclude all saving or storing? Assuredly not. It forbids nothing which does not interfere with present duty. It precludes nothing which does not indicate mistrust of God, and beget fearfulness and depression of spirit. Any planning or storing of this kind is not for him who prays this prayer. Any anxiety which says, What shall I eat? as if there would be no God to-morrow; any thought of the unknown future which weakens us in any way for plain, present duty; and any self-confident storing, as if we had really more in our barns and banks than in the resources of God; all these are certainly precluded. That there is a great difference between faithless, anxious imagining and scheming, and godly prudence, every one understands who has given a thought to the matter. From the former one sometimes wakes up, thoroughly ashamed of it. Have I work for to-day, and strength for to-day? Then let not thought of to-morrow's food, or how I shall get through to-morrow's duties, interfere with to-day's duties, which require for themselves all my thought and care. Let me *prepare* for to-morrow, so far as I can consistently with what I am called on to do to-day. Let me, for example, lay up seven years' corn, like Joseph, if I am given to understand there will be need of it. Let me, like our Lord himself, gather up the fragments of to-day, that nothing be lost for to-morrow. Let me lay by whatever will in all human probability be needed for simple maintenance; but let me do this, knowing that I am as dependent as ever on God, and let me do it only in so far as it does not clash with present claims of charity, hospitality, or station.

This, of course, is one of the cases in which a man's own conscience must draw the line; must say how much he is to spend or give, and how much to set against a future call. There is no other rule than his own conscience to define this. But of the principle on which all are to act, no one will be left in doubt who is from day to day sincerely asking God for his daily bread. And of the two extremes, trusting in gold to the utter exclusion of all confidence in God, and trusting in God to the neglect of the rules of prudence which He has taught, (which God calls "tempting Him,") no one needs to be told which is the more dangerous, and few can safely dispense with self-delivered warnings against it.

The answer, therefore, to this petition will be, that our spirits will be cleansed from worldliness, covetousness, and hardness of heart; from high-mindedness, self-confidence, and dishonesty; from discontent, envy, and indolence; and that we shall be enabled, without repining at what is past, or fretting ourselves with thoughts of the future, (though repenting of the past and preparing for the future,) to summon all the powers given us to this day's duty. And as we learn our place as dependents, we shall awake to the value of what is consigned to us, and as we commit the past and the future alike to God, there remains before us this day, a portion competent to our faculties, and practicable, with no uncertainties to distract us from the "valuable certainties" of the present. And this dependence should not be found difficult by those who have an Advocate such as ours, who well understands human necessities, Himself having hungered; whose earnest, purposing, and planning love ist he same now as when He "became poor that we might be rich," and who has so opened His riches to our poverty, that sufficiency *is* found in Him—every hungering soul finding enough in Him, every weary soul finding rest in Him, every tossed and breaking soul forgetting its sorrow in Him.

VI.

" And forgive us our debts, as we forgive our debtors."

No one who uses this prayer can be surprised to find that to the petition for bodily sustenance and the regulation of our earthly life, it is immediately added, *" And* forgive us our debts, as we forgive our debtors." To ask for more puts us in mind of what we have already received. To request the greatest favours from one who may give or withhold at pleasure, forces us to consider our claim, and calculate the probability of our being heard. And if our conduct towards any one has been unworthy, never does conscience make more painful mention of this than when circumstances bring us to acknowledge that we are dependent on this person. Nothing but sheer necessity will induce us to seek the good-will, or implore the aid of one whose past favours we have abused, whose person we have insulted, and of whose excellence and power we cherish a

grudging and irritable dislike, rather than a frank
and cordial admiration; but if necessity bids us
seek the presence and favour of such, we cannot
do so without at least a form of apology, which,
though it be not willing nor true, is yet understood to be requisite, and felt to be humbling.
Prudence prescribes, though penitence do not
prompt. But there are cases in which the aid
we seek is so vital, the gift we receive so
munificent, that stiff and hardened pride gives
way before genuine humility and contrite gratitude.

And so it is when we ask from God our daily
bread. "Continue us in life," we say to God;
and (not from heaven but) from within there
comes an answering voice, "Why should God
continue us in life? Is it to cumber His
ground; to take up room others might better
occupy; to waste His goodness and abuse His
forbearance?" Give me this day my bread; but
why to *me?* Am I so useful, so grateful, so
considerate? To *me;* to whom is it I attract
the regard of God when I use these words?
"Give me *this* day my bread;" and why *this*
day? Is it because yesterday was so well spent?
Were all my duties yesterday so discharged that

I can with some assurance ask another day ? As every moment of it was charged with something from God, was there on my part an unbroken rendering to God of His due ?   Do I find in yesterday reasons for God's maintaining me to-day, far outweighing whatever might induce Him to withdraw His support ? or, conscious of some deficiency, do I say, " Give me this new day," that I may have some chance of paying off the debt I have contracted ; that I may this 'day do more than my duty, and have a surplus to set over against yesterday's deficit ? Who needs to be told that such hopes are vain, that all we can this day perform is already due ; that we cannot limit our service to God, nor by greater diligence part of the day free the remainder from all claim ; that we cannot serve Him so many hours, and then say, " Now I have done enough, now I may cease rendering obedience to God ? "   All that we have for to-day is needed for to-day; it cannot overflow to to-morrow, nor make up for the lack of yesterday.   If we misspent yesterday's bread, we must to-day simply ask forgiveness ; if we ran into God's debt yesterday by omission or transgression, then to-day we cannot make up for that, but must ask His free pardon.   And the more we seek for some reason for God's giving us this day's bread, the more do we discover reason for God's calling us to account for what we have already received. Our "give" must ever be followed by "forgive." The goodness of God leads us to repentance. He overcomes our evil with His good, and never more forcibly reminds us of our ungracious past than when the present shines with His grace.

The linking of this petition to the preceding shows us further that forgiveness is a vital thing, as needful for our daily life as the bread it is here connected with. Forgiveness is as much the basis of a day's duty as bread. If we are to serve on earth, we must have bread; but if we are to serve either on earth or elsewhere, we must have forgiveness. As surely as we faint and die without bread, so surely do we faint and die from all godly life, and for all godly purposes, if we have not forgiveness. Bread supplies the personal capability and outward opportunity of doing the things which please God : forgiveness supplies the inward condition in which a man can do anything pleasing to God. Until the matter of sin is finally adjusted, and an understanding come to on this point between God and the soul, there is

9

no willingness, no heartiness, no constancy, nor any acceptance of service. To serve God from any other motive than love has been proved impossible by the lives of so many, that words need not be spent upon the matter. And that a man cannot love God while he is heavily and inexcusably and hopelessly in His debt, is what no one needs to be told who is really seeking for information about service. I know this. Yes; but do I act upon my knowledge, or does not my knowledge condemn my practice? Do I begin each day with a spirit free, unburdened, and lively, running in the way of God's commandments, as the healthy body delights not in sluggish sauntering, but in vigorous and difficult exercise? As I often take it for granted that the bread will come of itself without any provident interposition of God, do I not also many a day pass by the forgiveness of God as if it would come of itself? But if it comes at all, it comes at my request. And if it do not come to-day, then this day is lost—lost for the service and glorifying of Him who gives it, and lost for my own best good. For as bread not only satisfies the appetite which the past has begotten, but also gives strength for time to come, so forgiveness not only clears away what the past has accumulated, but lays the foundation for what is to come. And other foundation than this there is none, as little as there is any way of sustaining life besides eating and drinking. We can as little discover some elixir which shall work in our spirits the same charm as forgiveness, as we can discover some specific or private means of sustaining our bodies, which shall put us beyond the necessity of taking meat like other men. And therefore are we to be sure that we are obtaining this forgiveness, this daily spiritual nourishment; not using this petition lightly, as if we could live quite as well unforgiven as forgiven; as if it would make very little difference whether this day be spent in God's favour or under His displeasure.

And how would God have us view our sins when we seek their forgiveness? As debts. To get at the full iniquity of sin, we need to consider it in various lights; and so in Scripture we find it designated by a variety of names, each of which suggests some peculiar quality of sin. It springs into life from such opposite parts of our nature, and gathers strength from so many different motives; its heinousness is darkened by so many aggravations, and its consequences run out in so many directions, that it is impossible to gather up all its evil and express it in a single word. Sometimes it is transgression or trespass, and here we see our reckless wickedness in departing from the straight path of God's commandments, the "everlasting way" that runs on eternally into deeper blessedness. Sometimes it is rebellion against God, as if we took delight in going contrary to Him, irrespective of any pleasure or profit apparently to be gained. And sometimes it is folly, showing us the weakness of our hearts, and their proneness to be deluded, and to miss the aim and end of our being. But when we confess, we are helped by viewing them as debts; an expression which leads us to consider, not so much the evil dispositions from which our sins proceeded, as the relation to God in which they have left us. And manifestly it is this which is most appropriate to be on our minds, (and which, in truth, must be on our minds,) when we come before God to ask His forgiveness. This view of sin takes us and sets us down in our true position before God as His debtors. It throws into my soul the confession, "I am connected with God, and the connexion is—debt." It is not a word which directly points to the moral evil of sin, but it very distinctly declares the position of the sinner. It may not be that view of sin which most powerfully excites repentance ; it is not introspection nor self-loathing which it most directly induces ; but it is a word which shows that our sins have to do with more than ourselves, which shows that they have connected me with God, which speaks of God and myself in the same word, and at the same time exhibits the relation I presently hold to God. And this is just what we need to see clearly when we pray for pardon ; that we are debtors, not only miserable sinners, whose pitiable case may well move God to compassion, but His servants who, in sinning and ruining themselves, have been most grievously wronging and defrauding Him, and whose sins have done as much injury (so He represents it) to Him as to themselves.

Sin, then, is a personal matter between myself and God. My sins have been affecting God. It has been a matter that He has considered, and He has noted a difference when I have done one thing rather than another. He has been expecting, waiting for service at my hand. At great cost He has furnished me with valuable aids and instruments, wherewith to further His purposes; and these I have abused, squandered, or destroyed. Again and again He has renewed my equipment as His servant, never casting me off as hopeless, but carefully adjusting my circumstances, so as to make opportunities of good easy, and what have I rendered Him again? All my life I have been receiving at His hand; "what have I that I have not received?" What should I have, were He to withdraw all the support He is now affording me? What should I be, were He suddenly to banish me beyond His power? And for all I receive, (which I can as soon number the hairs of my head as reckon,) He expects a return. What return have I made? I hear His voice demanding of me, " What owest thou to thy Lord?" I cannot tell; I have never so much as known what I owed: have seldom so much as tried to form a careful, true, and honest estimate of what is due from me to Him; have seldom set myself against the known deceitfulness of sin, and determined that, at least, I should have a clear, definite understanding of what I owe to God, and endeavour, as the one thing which, at all events and at any cost, must be done by my life, to discharge what is due to God, to whom I owe all.

"Debt" is a designation of sin which calls to mind a large class of sins, which we are very prone to forget in seeking pardon—sins of omission. These have no palpable and visible existence, such as glaring acts of sin possess. While they rival positive acts of wrong-doing in their iniquity, they outrival them in their power of eluding conscience. So that, if there be a man who, when he draws near to God with the purpose of confessing, is at a loss what to say; whose eye, as it turns back to scrutinise his life, is arrested by no startling forms of iniquity, is not glazed with terror, nor sinks in shame from the ghastly phantoms that pursue him, and stretch forth quick and strong hands of vengeance to seize him; let him look once more over that wide and void expanse, and let him turn upon himself and ask what there ought to be there. Let him say to his soul, Ought there to be nothing more than you see? Was it to do nothing more than you have done, that God gave you this life, and made you what you are? Have you done all for yourself that you could, so that now you are as like to Christ as possible? Have you done all for others that you could, so that none are hungering now, who might have been fed by you; none in sorrow now, whom a word or deed of yours might have relieved; none in bitterness of spirit or enmity against you now, whom a slight humiliation on your part might have saved from sin; none mistaken as to the character of Christ and His religion, who might have known differently had you done what you could?

But there is one sin of omission that rises up * from every part of our life, and fills with condemnation the expanse which, to the careless eye, might seem vacant. There is one debt incurred which fills the soul with new and keener shame, however overwhelmed it has been already with a sense of sin. God's "unspeakable gift" has been abused by us. He has spent all upon us, the whole resources of Deity, all that made this world and more,† all the wisdom, and the glory, and all (if we may say "all" of what has proved itself infinite) the love of God. Only when we can fathom the humiliation of Christ, only when

---

* As at the resurrection men will rise from empty wastes, where it would not have been suspected that any were concealed, let a man look back on all his omissions, and think what the divine law can raise from them against him."— FOSTER's *Lectures*, vol. i., p. 348.

† This idea will be found elaborated in the *Patience of Hope*, with the usual felicity of the authoress.

we can understand what is contained in that expression "He emptied Himself," only when we
can measure the interval between the throne of
God and the tomb in Joseph's garden, between
"the living God" and a dead man, shall we be
able to measure God's gift to us and our debt to
Him. And is the world to go on as if the Son
of God had never been its inhabitant? Has
Christ done all this for us, and is no return
expected from us? Is all this to be done before
us, and no new feelings to arise in our hearts, no
new and wider thoughts, no lasting alteration of
conduct? Can one act so closely in our interest,
and our relation to Him be as it was? Let us
take our stand before the cross, where we may
see the freeness of God's giving at its height,
and, standing there, let us say if we have rendered to Him His due. Call sin debt to Christ,
and the matter is brought to a very simple issue.
Had I myself spent my all upon another, put
aside my own interest and prospects, and given
my whole life and labour to him; had I, in that
life, met with the sorest trouble on his account,
and yet never turned aside, and had I been
tempted by the most alluring openings for myself, and yet held the interest of the object of

this life-long sacrifice so close to my heart, that I preferred bitterness and disgrace for him, to pleasure and profit for myself; and had this resulted in a successful issue, had I achieved prosperity and secure satisfaction for him, should I expect no return, should I not expect so much as some extra thought and regard; nay, would it not be the most unaccountable ingratitude if he did not become my firmest friend, the man on whom I could always count? How the world would hoot such a man; how the world would scorn his excuses! And is all changed when I myself am that man, and Jesus Christ the self-sacrificing friend? Is all changed because the sacrifice becomes greater than the most laborious words can describe, and the blessing conferred increasingly rich through eternity? Can our hearts really deceive us thus; can any blindness leave unobserved our debt to Jesus Christ?

But for all our debts, what does God demand of us? Are His demands anything like those of the human law of debt, of that old law which claimed the person of the debtor, and handed him over to his creditor, to be cut in pieces if he chose; to be sold with his family and effects, if he chose; to be chained to a life of drudgery, if

such were the will of his creditor? Are we at
least to suffer some penalty, to feel for a while
something of the bitterness of that poverty to
which we have brought another? Not so. All
that is asked is, that we acknowledge the debt,
and accept of its remission. And what else can
we do? We can find no way of evading our
creditor: "Though they dig into hell, thence
shall mine hand take them; though they climb
up to heaven, thence will I bring them down;
and though they hide themselves in Carmel, I
will search and take them out thence; and
though they be hid from my sight in the bottom
of the sea, thence will I command the serpent,
and he shall bite them." It is not, then, by any
evasion of ours that our debts can be got rid of;
neither will they pass away by any forgetfulness
or waiting of ours. They are not fancies, which
the changes of life may put to flight. They are
not mere names or suppositions which need not
be regarded. They are real; entered in the
book of God's remembrance to the utmost far-
thing. We cannot live our lives over again; the
sins are committed; the debts are contracted.
We cannot now make up for what we have
already done wrong and left undone. All our

strength is needed for our present duty. The future will do well, if it keeps itself solvent. But "ask, and ye shall receive." "The word is nigh thee, even in thy mouth and in thy heart;" will not the heart send to the lips this one petition, "Forgive me my debts?"

For pardon is one of the things that we can only have by asking. It is a thing which must come from another, from Him, namely, whom we have wronged. It is His to forgive, and nothing we can do can earn it. We cannot pass a free pardon upon ourselves, remit the debts we owe to another, absolve ourselves. But God, whom we have offended, and in whose debt we are, says, we may have pardon for the asking. "There is forgiveness with God;" and were there not forgiveness with Him, then to look for it elsewhere were absurd, for He being the party offended can alone forgive the offence. Forgiveness is with Him, not as being provided by another, and now put into His power to administer, but as it is dependent on His will solely, whether there shall be any such thing as forgiveness of sin or not. All provision that could be made for our pardon, and all administration of that pardon now, must of necessity depend on and origi-

nate in the will of God. And that will is, that
we be freely pardoned. And this being so, it is
deep dishonour we do to God's will and word, if
we say or think that something must be added
to the simplicity of this petition, or that we are
not to expect any very wonderful results from
this prayer. These words are something more
than an appropriate acknowledgment that we
owe God much, they are not a charm by the
mere repetition of which we win God's favour;
they are the petition of the soul for what we do
need and can only have from God.

But how does God himself encourage us to
use this petition in faith? He puts into our
mouths these words, "as we forgive our debtors."
And for our encouragement, first of all, these
words are surely given us. For here we have
the same argument as is elsewhere expanded in
that marvellous verse which is instinct with persuasion, and which, as often as we read it, re-
kindles our faith: "If ye, being evil, know how
to give good gifts unto your children, how much
more shall your heavenly Father give the Holy
Spirit to them that ask him?" Here, with like
force of reasoning, we are taught to say to God:
If we, being evil, can forgive our debtors, how

much more may we expect forgiveness of Thee, whose name is love, who art our heavenly Father, with whom there is forgiveness, and who hast made Thyself known as "ready to forgive?" And to set us on the firmest ground, and in an absolutely unassailable position, when we thus pray, there comes further in aid of our plea the idea which God himself has given us of human forgiveness; and we plead with still greater power, "If on us who are full of wickedness, and in whom malice and bitterness congenially dwell, Thou Thyself hast laid the injunction to forgive seventy times seven, if our brother offend, what limit dare we put to Thy forgiveness, which is high above ours as heaven is above the earth?" Certainly this is a strong argument which God puts into our lips. Will not He do more than He has commanded us to do? Are we not to expect more from Him than from one another? Well may our Lord add, "For if *ye* forgive men their trespasses, your heavenly Father will forgive you."

This clause, appended to our appeal for pardon does not exhaust the reasons there are for assurance of success; we might be encouraged by many other considerations. The likelihood of our obtaining what we ask is grounded on the actual and abundant provision that has been made for our forgiveness, on the express offers of God, and on a number of circumstances made known in Scripture ; but the likelihood that is here alone considered is that which arises from the nature of the person appealed to. It is simply God's matchless readiness to forgive that we here use for our encouragement. We are reminded by the words we use that we are now appealing to one, the forgivingness of whose character is such, that He has impressed this attribute of His distinctly upon His law, and has commanded that, in order to please Him, it is but necessary that we be loving and forgiving. And nothing can more effectually maintain within us the confident boldness which He desires, than thus to understand the infinite depth of love and length of forbearance that reside in Him with whom we deal, and on whose mercy we hang. It is (need it be said ?) very fitting that before we approach God, we should distinctly understand how forgiveness has been prepared for us, and should, by the contemplation of the infinite merit and inexhaustible efficacy of the blood of Christ, encourage ourselves to draw near to Him by whose judgment we stand or fall; but when we actually stand in His presence, and are at length explicitly asking Him for pardon, no encouragement can be more fitting than that which arises from a deep impression of the forgiving nature to which our appeal is made, and nothing can more promptly and effectually create this impression than the remembrance, that forgivingness of disposition is enjoined upon *us* by God as the prime requisite of character, and that His one commandment is that we love one another. And it is this remembrance which these words of the prayer recall as often as we utter them with understanding.

But is this an encouragement that all of us can use? Have we in heart accepted the seventy times seven as our rule, and do we desire to be found in its practice? Dare we thus reason from ourselves to God? Dare we point God to our conduct, and say, " As we forgive, so forgive us?" The words of the petition assure us that whatever may stand in the way of our forgiveness, it certainly is not this, that God is a hard judge who would rather condemn than acquit. But then they remind us of this, only by reminding us that even we ourselves, imperfect though we be, delight rather in the forgiveness than in the punishment of our enemy. But is this the fact ? Of course we expect God's forgiveness to be of a very different measure from our own ; but have we any forgivingness of spirit, even "according to the measure of a man," from which we can take courage to hope in the wide and perfect and infinite forgivingness of God ? Have we the little from which we can reason to God's much ? Or are not some, when they use this prayer, in danger of turning it into an imprecation ? Is it not true that many of us are in danger of uttering that most terrible curse upon ourselves, which has been put into language and named "the prayer of the unforgiving man ?"* "O God, I have sinned against Thee many times from my youth up until now. I have often been forgetful of Thy goodness ; I have not duly thanked Thee for Thy mercies ; I have neglected Thy service ; I have broken Thy laws ; I have done many things utterly wrong against Thee. All this I know ; and beside this doubtless I have committed many secret sins, which in my blindness I have failed to notice. Such is my guiltiness, O Lord, in Thy sight ; deal with me, I beseech Thee, even as I deal with my neighbour. He has

* By A. W. Hare.

o1

not offended me one-tenth, one-hundredth part as much as I have offended Thee; but he has offended me very grievously, and I cannot forgive him. Deal with me, I beseech Thee, O Lord, as I deal with him. He has been very ungrateful to me, though not a tenth, not a hundredth part as ungrateful as I have been to Thee; yet I cannot overlook such base and shameful ingratitude. Deal with me, I beseech Thee, O Lord, as I deal with him. I remember and treasure up every little trifle, which shows how ill he has behaved to me. Deal with me, I beseech Thee, O Lord, as I deal with him. I am determined to take the very first opportunity of doing him an ill turn. Deal with me, I beseech Thee, O Lord, as I deal with him."

The encouragement of this petition, then, is not a mere commonplace which any one may safely use. A true cordial it is, but if applied to the wrong condition may prove deleterious and deadly. The boldness we have before God must not be the superficial presumption of sentiment-alism, but it must be of a piece with the tenor of our life. For there is one thing we need in prayer as much as encouragement, and that is sincerity. We must be thrown back upon our

real desires. That encouragement which is not
backed by our true state of heart, and which does
not consist with our conduct, is mere delusion.
The only right confidence before God is that
which the apostle commends, and which can only
be enjoyed "when our own hearts condemn us
not;" that is, when we ask God, not for those
things which we know we ought to desire, but for
those things which are ever floating before our
hopes, and drawing forth our heart's affections,
and the efforts of our lives. If it is a fictitious
desire, or a desire got up for propriety's sake,
which we present before God, our hearts condemn
us, and we have no confidence. And what is to
be carefully marked as the key to the encouragement in this petition is this : that in point of
fact every one who is set upon obtaining forgiveness does forgive his neighbour, and therefore
every one who uses the petition in sincerity, in
the truth of the heart, as the expression of the
fixed bent of his soul, does receive the encouragement which is laid up in the appended clause.
This encouragement is not for those who have a
merely occasional and passing impression of their
need of forgiveness ; it is not for those who prize
God's favour to-day, but to-morrow forget it ; it

is not for the insincere, who hold this petition as a veil between God and their souls; nor for the double-minded, who love this life, but would also secure themselves against the next. It is not for any who can thoughtlessly and almost flippantly ejaculate this petition merely from the lip; but it is for all on whose heart God reads the deeply cut consciousness of their immeasurable debt, and the earnest and abiding desire for pardon.

This appended clause has, therefore, a twofold use. Wrapt up in its encouragement there is a check to conscience. We are not to be allowed to present the petition at all, unless it be from the deepest sense of our need, and of the greatness of the gift we seek; a sense which is in reality equivalent to true repentance, and which brings with it, as its uniform and necessary fruit, love to our neighbour. And every one who knows how apt we are to become either hypocrites or careless formalists in prayer, will recognise the suitableness of such a check, and will appreciate the propriety of its being appended to this petition rather than any other. For this, more than any other, has been a lip-deep petition, and has been shamefully abused by self-satisfied or careless petitioners, by ourselves when we ask forgiveness, as we often ask it, without any considerate remembrance of the cost of it, thinking it the easiest thing for God to give, and forgetting that this has been prepared for us at a far greater expense, at a more personal expense, than anything else we can implore. It has been the endeavour of many teachers to persuade us, and yet we need to be reminded, that a word could create and beautify a world, and "an act of will bestow it upon us," but it has cost God the humiliation and suffering of His well-beloved Son to grant the boon which now we ask. And therefore we are here suddenly startled out of all dreamy and indifferent prayer, and are aroused by being brought face to face with our own real desires and our own real life; we are reminded that our prayer had far better be unsaid, if it is not of a piece with our state of heart; that we cannot pray as one person and live as another; that we do not look as earnestly as we ought for the remission of our debts, (and therefore need not expect it,) unless we be doing what we can to avoid contracting new ones; that, in short, we have no encouragement whatever to present this petition, unless conscience assures us that the love of God, on wnich we hope, has entered our souls and changed them, and has become the principle and law of our lives.

All difficulty vanishes from this clause, once we recognise the point of fact, that a man humbled before God is invariably and necessarily charitable to his neighbour. The spirit of pride and the spirit of hatred are one; they stand and fall together. Do I find it hard to forgive the little offences of my fellow-servant, the few pence he owes me? Then do I, indeed, understand what it is I ask God to do, when I ask Him to cancel that debt of mine of ten thousand talents? For how can I have the heart to challenge another with his offences against me, when my own misdeed and sin against God is pressing upon my soul, and forcing me to cry for pardon? Myself helpless and keenly sensible that I am utterly dependent on the forbearance and free grace of God, alive to the shamefulness of my wrong-doing against Him, and crying for mere mercy without a shadow of hope that I can make the slightest reparation, I cannot, I really cannot, harbour hard and unforgiving thoughts against my neighbour, nor insist upon my claims. The words of the evangelist Mark are therefore by no

means alarming to one who really longs for pardon
of his great debt, though they, even more distinctly than the words of Matthew, require that,
before receiving the forgiveness of God, we forgive
others. He quotes our Lord as saying, " When
ye stand praying, forgive, if ye have aught against
any; that your Father also, which is in heaven,
may forgive you your trespasses. But if ye do
not forgive, neither will your Father which is in
heaven forgive your trespasses." As if he said,
" Your act of forgiveness must precede the act
you hope that God will perform." There is something standing in the way of your forgiveness,
which you must remove. Something is to be
done before God can forgive you, which you
must do. But, then, it is a thing which you
cannot but be doing, if you are compelled to
seek God's forgiveness from any just sense of
your own sin. For just in proportion as your
own sin against God appears great, so will the
offences of others against yourself appear small.
It is not that our forgivingness of spirit wins the
forgiveness of God, but that our unforgivingness
cannot accept the forgiveness of God. By forgiving others we do not earn our own forgiveness, but most assuredly we cannot receive that

forgiveness until we forgive others. We are not prepared to seek it; we have not seen our own great debt, and are merely asking God for we know not what, unless humility and joy in the hope of God's pardon have excluded from our hearts all malice against our neighbour.

So that this clause merely forms a demand that, when we ask God for forgiveness, we shall know what we ask for. If we know what we ask for, we will ask it, and cannot but ask it, in the spirit here required. We come approving the law of forgiveness; it is all our hope for ourselves, and we act upon it towards others. With divine skill and kindness these words, which we are to repeat as often as we ask forgiveness, bid us think how great a gift we seek, and forbid us to deceive ourselves with a merely verbal petition, and so to defraud ourselves of God's pardon. They refuse to let us near God, until we realise the vastness of His gift, and are prepared to claim it. When we feel unable sincerely to use this petition, we are not to turn our attention to our neighbour, and endeavour to kindle love in our hearts by extenuating his offences and magnifying his good deeds. Not at all. We are to bend our thoughts to our own state, to count up our

debts to God, to set them in the light of His coun-
tenance, and thus measuring our own great debt,
and learning that marvellous love which gives
ground of hope even to such debtors, our hearts
drink in a humility, a peace, and a joy with which
hardness towards our fellow-men cannot dwell.
And so invariably does the one feeling flow from
the other, that we may learn the presence of the
one from the fact of the other's presence. An
infallible test is thus graciously put into our
hands, by which we may learn whether we are
asking enough from God. If there is still in our
hearts any bitterness towards man, then there is
too little desire for pardon. If there is too vivid
a consciousness of our claims upon others, there
is too low an estimate of God's claims upon us.
If the wrong done us by others seems greater
than we can forgive and forget, then our own
wrong-doing is affecting us less than it should;
the mind of God and our mind still view very
different objects, when our sins are spoken of.
But God would fully pardon us, He would not
have us live with a single debt uncancelled, and
therefore He gives us a test by which we may
always learn whether, when we use this petition,
we are indeed seeking that all our great debt be

forgiven. He gives us these words, certainly not to make our prayer impossible, but to preserve us from verbally asking for what He would have us seek with our whole soul; and because He would have us, indeed, receive what we ask, when we say, "Forgive us our debts."

> "Alas! alas!
> Why, all the souls that were, were forfeit once,
> And He that might the vantage best have took
> Found out the remedy. How would you be,
> If He, which is the top of judgment, should
> But judge you as you are? Oh! think on that;
> And mercy then will breathe within your lips,
> Like man new made."

VII.

"And lead us not into temptation, but deliver us from evil."

OUR prayer, then, is not finished, when we have cast upon our Father in heaven all the cares of our earthly life, and have been also freed from the burden of our sins. It is pleasant to sit in God's smile, and gather strength in the assurance of His favour, but the future frowns terribly upon us, and we quail at the remembrance that we are still surrounded by the world we have renounced, and are still liable to the sins we have just deplored. Acknowledged as the children of God, we do not yet enjoy the security of his home; and it is when we look forward and see what lies between us and that home, that we become aware that sin has not only stained but poisoned us ; that the burden has not only wearied but weakened us ; that the debt has not only hampered but demoralised us. It will not do to rest in the quiet calm of forgiveness, as if we had now attained that for which we were apprehended. "Thy sins be forgiven thee" is followed forthwith not by "well done, good and faithful servant, enter thou into the joy of thy Lord," but by "go and sin no more." But this "go," what a bleak and dangerous world does it launch us into; to what possibilities of disaster and hurt, to what likelihood of ruin does it dismiss us! How contradictory * it seems to add "sin no more." We cannot but turn and say, "Do thou, then, Lord, lead us; and lead us not into temptation."

And as we continue to pray daily for forgiveness, and find that it is mostly the same sins we have to confess, and how the appetite that is in us for evil finds food in the most unexpected and unlikely quarters, the sense of our weakness grows, and we should feel the prayer to be insufficient for us, did not our fears find some hope in it, and our feebleness some security. Like those who have received a precious charge to convey safely through a country infested with enemies, undermined with pitfalls, or reeking with malaria, we go forth with spirits made rich by the favour of God, to traverse that dangerous interval between this present moment and our complete redemption. We fear to step out into

* This idea occurs in a recent volume of devotional poetry.

the ways of this world, lest our garments, made white in the blood of the Lamb, be again defiled. The world has not changed to suit our condition. We would not now sin as once we did, but the world will still be as pressing in its offers of easy helps to sin, as ever it was. There are our former companions in sin waiting for us to join them again; there are our old haunts, and the old seasons come round as before, and our familiar sins meet us again, and tell us that all things are ready. They take the words of wisdom, and say, "Come, eat of my bread, and drink of the wine which I have mingled." The same business awaits us, in which heretofore we have found such room for sinning; the same hours of leisure, and the same pleasant ways of spending these. All remains the same, ready as ever to make our old course easy, but with no sympathy for our new condition, no rejoicing with us over our new-found treasure, no friendly desire to enter into and prosper our new views. All the world is as it was, and what disappoints us more than all, there is still in us too much that remains as it was. The spirit indeed is willing, but the flesh is weak as ever. It is still flesh. It is still so adapted to what the world offers, that it clamours to be satisfied in the world's way, hints that we wrong ourselves and undergo unnecessary hardships in striving to subdue it, and that it cannot be very criminal to do what our nature demands, and what our circumstances not only permit, but induce and almost drive us to.

Those who have nothing to lose are (to a proverb) little put about by the presence of thieves; and of those whose hopes are small, the fears also are few and slight. The fear of defilement found no place in our souls, until the grateful sense of purity introduced it. It seemed a small thing to risk all temptation, before we experienced the peace and joy of the goodwill of God; but now that we have tasted His goodness, and prize His favour as our choicest possession, it seems a hazardous thing to venture into a sea of temptations, one or other of which will almost inevitably sweep over our soul, and leave it bare of its prize under the displeasure of God. I do not purpose to sin; I have no present and special resolve which I know to be wrong, but am I therefore secure? Or has it not often happened with me that, when least I expected it, evil was very powerfully present with me? Besides sinning deliberately, have I not sinned through ignorance, through weakness, through surprise, through habit? Did I not sin, because I was tempted by such a combination of inducements, and hedged off from the right path by so many difficulties, that I greatly fear to be placed again in a similar predicament? Rather will I pray, "Lead me not into temptation, but deliver me from evil."

A person may use these words as two distinct petitions; but, as they here stand, they are connected and form one double request. It is one utterance of the soul. The soul does not first view temptation and utter its desire about this, and then view evil, and utter a new desire about that; but seeing at one view temptation and evil, and knowing, moreover, how they are joined together, a prayer is uttered which, though it has two parts, is one. There is no end that we can propose for ourselves short of deliverance from evil, and no means can be suggested as more necessary to the attainment of this than being kept from temptation. To be kept from disease, from poverty, from loss of friends, from any ill that the soul dreads, would not be so broad and effectual a petition as this, if our end be deliverance from evil. From these and all other ills we desire deliverance; but if there be left within us evil dispositions that will respond to temptation, then there is no lasting deliverance for us. For this is the account of the whole matter which is given by the apostle James: "Every man is tempted when he is drawn away of his own lust and enticed. Then when lust hath conceived, it bringeth forth sin, and sin when it is finished, bringeth forth death." Evil, then, is that to which temptation leads, and to which sin binds. And there is that in every one of us which, if left to itself, will bring us to the most evil form of evil. Only let it have its way, only take no precautions against it, and gradually the evil within will wed the evil without, and death will grow up around you. This will as certainly result as death will result, if you place an animal that lives by breath into a poisoned atmosphere.

But if the evil be within us, how will a merely negative petition effect our cure? How will the mere absence of certain outward objects destroy the evil that has its life within the soul? It will do so by taking from that evil the food on which its life depends. Fire must have fuel, must be active, in order to be living; it may smoulder long, but die it must, if it be not fed. And so it is of evil dispositions and propensities. Give

them no opportunity, let neither sense nor imagination minister to them by presenting their
objects, and, finding no outlet, they will pine and
die. This at least is the grand external means
of deliverance from evil. Plant a tree in a con-
genial soil, and surround it with every advantage,
it will grow and bear fruit after its kind ; and
just as certainly will our desires find nourishment in the world we are in, and so grow up to
matured sins, and bring forth death, if they be
not checked. And therefore we pray that God
would not suffer the nourishment suitable to our
fleshly and natural desires to be given, but would
so order our circumstances that we shall have
the least possible temptation to sin ; that we
may be put in positions in which there is least
opportunity of gratifying those of our inclinations
to sin which are strongest, and in which our
opposite tendencies may be most easily and
effectually matured. Here the experience of our
better mind arms itself against the law of the
members. We take precautions against ourselves.

The first question that rises in most minds
concerning this petition is, " Is there any likelihood that God would lead us into temptation, or
why do we pray that He would not ? " Is it not

said that as God is not tempted, so neither tempteth He any? But we do not present this petition because we suppose that God ever stands on the side of evil, and allures us to sin. This would be something more than leading into temptation. What God often does, what He did in the case of Abraham, of Job, and especially of our Lord himself, is to expose a man in a very critical and precarious position, to bring him in the course of his life into circumstances where sin is very easy, holiness very difficult. We read that it was "of the Spirit" that "Jesus was led up into the wilderness to be tempted of the devil;" a very instructive intimation, giving us in one view all the parties concerned. The human nature, with its liability to temptation, its capability to suffer and to enjoy; the divine nature, ordering the circumstances which may permit the temptation to take place; and the diabolical nature, *the* tempter, exerting his utmost to induce sin. (For this is the distinguishing characteristic of Satan, that he desires that sin may be the result of every temptation.) Our Lord had just passed through His own trial, when He gave this prayer to His disciples. He remembered what it had cost Him, how His noly nature had seemed to be violently driven within sight of sin, and He knew that were His disciples to be similarly exposed, the result might be defeat instead of victory. It is He knows best what temptation is, and who has most successfully overcome it, that bids us pray, "Lead us not into temptation." It became His own prayer before He entered on that greatest of all temptations, "Father, if it be possible, let this cup pass from me." And how is this, that we see the soul of Jesus trembling in prospect of temptation, while we brave it, fearlessly, confidently, and even boastfully? He knows what Satan's power is, and He knows the evil of sin. And he who has some measure of the spirit of Christ, and fears above all else the Father's displeasure, will not go forth believing that he is proof against every assault of Satan or the world, but will pray that God will so guide his path that he may escape from those more violent or seductive temptations to which he sees others yielding. He will not seek to change this petition into "succour us when tempted," but, out of the consciousness of his own weakness, desires rather to avoid temptation than to take the chances of overcoming it.

And this raises a second question, " Can I pray
thus with any hope, seeing that life is just one
series of temptations ? " Must we not meet temptations, whether we deprecate them or no ? Is
there any such man on earth as an untempted
man ? Can God give us what we ask for, and
still keep us on this earth ? How shall He guide
us ? Is there any course through life free from
all inducement to sin ? Where shall He put us ?
Is there any position where we shall no longer
need constant vigilance, unflinching constancy,
and painful effort of soul ? " Lead me not into
temptation," how do I expect that this will be
answered ? Is there some profession the members of which find nothing in it to foster their
own corrupt affections ? Is there some employment in which failure shall no more tempt us to
murmur, nor success elate us to forgetfulness of
God ? We know that, be a man's occupation
what it may, he cannot be secure from all entice-
ment. Various indeed are the temptations that
assail men, from the statesman, whose name is in
every man's mouth, to the invalid whom the
world has long forgotten ; but every one can tell
of some part of his lot that seems bordering on
evil, from which at any moment he could pass

over into sin, and at which he is in constant
danger of being urged by a sudden impulse
across the boundary. Every one can tell of
something in his occupation that seems to con-
spire with something in his character, and make
sinning easier to him there than elsewhere. He
is passionate, and there is some constant source
of irritation; or he is covetous, and there is an
unrighteous, but prolific source of gain always
offering itself. He is ambitious, and there is a
path open to its gratification, which would also
lead him to sin; or he loves the applause of men,
and that desire can be gratified. He is naturally despondent and distrustful, and he is called
to endure protracted suffering; or he is naturally
careless and worldly, and he enjoys unmingled
prosperity. Or he is liable to sullenness, or
pride, or sensuality, or indolence, and whatever
be his infirmity, he will not be without drawings
that way, encouragements in his infirmity, opportunities of showing what manner of man he is.
And shall we therefore cease to use this petition?
We will all the more perseveringly use it. For
if temptations be so thickly strewn around us,
who shall say how soon we may be overtaken in
a fault? At first this petition may pass our lips

with no quite definite expectation. It only rises irrepressibly out of the sense of our own inability to cope with certain temptations. But as it is used from day to day, side by side with our daily life, it interprets itself more fully. We find in it the suitable expression of a desire that grows up within us, that, whilst we must be exposed to temptations, these may be proportioned to our strength; in other words, that God would keep us out of situations in which, so far as we can judge, it would be beyond our present strength to keep from sinning.

The harder we purpose in our souls to live to God, the more clearly do we see how we displease Him. We begin to take account of this, that there are certain conditions in which we almost invariably, if not invariably, sin, despite all our resolves to the contrary. We remember our resolves, nay, we remember how a few hours ago we besought pardon of similar sin, and yet we yield. There are persons whose company always betrays us into slandering, or scoffing, or bitter envy, or hypocrisy, or some evil passion; there are places in which we cannot maintain, or have at least never yet maintained, even our usual regard to the will of God, and from which we return less disposed than we ought to remember

Christ, or engage in any religious duty; there are books we read, or trains of thought we indulge in, which lower our tone and unhinge the mind for serious, vigorous, and devout exercise. Now it is very often the case, that it is quite at our option that we thus put ourselves in the way of temptation. It forms no part of our duty to ourselves or our friends thus to expose ourselves, and yet we find it very difficult to disentangle ourselves from the habits we have formed by a voluntary and repeated exposure to the same influences. So agreeable and fascinating have these situations or employments which tempt us become, that it is beyond our strength to give them up. Surely in this case we may ask God so to order our circumstances that these things may have less power of appeal than formerly. How the prayer may be answered we do not know. We may be removed to a distance from the companions or objects which most effectually tempted us; our attention may be strongly diverted to some pursuit which dulls for a time the other attraction, and breaks the habit we have formed. But how the answer shall come it is not for us to decide. God, in one way or other, may either make it a physical impossibility for us to be in the way of temptation, or He may add to our condition some balance, which keeps us from rushing into the arms of sin at every invitation. So that, whether the temptations we have reason to fear be in the way of our callings, or have been voluntarily and recklessly encountered by us, this petition is suitable ; and it will inevitably rise to our lips, if we be fearing sin.

But there is a third class of temptations against which we have urgent need to use this petition. There are sudden surprises, which neither occur in the ordinary duties of our employments, nor as we might have anticipated and taken precautions against, but emerge unexpectedly. A special importance attaches to these, for it is thus that many of our greatest sins have been committed ; and, when resisted, it is then that we have taken the greatest steps in advance Godwards. In short, these are the temptations in which, beyond all others, it is evident that God is making proof of us. To compare the temptation of David with that of Joseph, similar in kind, but so opposite in result; or that of Adam in the garden with that of Jesus in the wilderness, will sufficiently show us how critical these times are, against which we can use no precaution but this prayer, asking that God would not suffer us to be so assailed. Let a man choose some of his memorable sins, those that conscience needs not to search for, but keeps floating on the surface of the memory, and let him consider how it came about that he fell into these, and he shall find that in very many cases it was because he was suddenly tempted; an unexpected opportunity presented itself of doing what he had long desired to do, or of getting what he had often coveted, or of becoming what ambition or vanity had been set upon; and this opportunity did not offer itself bare, but well supported by inducements and incentives from every side. Was it an appeal to anger or hatred? Then something had first occurred to irritate or imbitter. Was it to licentiousness the allurement appealed? Then something had first occurred to excite. Was it to love of gain the temptation spoke? Then something had previously shown the desirableness of wealth, or taught the bitterness of poverty. Whatever it was that overran the soul and spoiled it, we think we could have resisted had the temptation come in some other shape, at some other time, when we had been under more wholesome influences; had there not, in short, been so many things conspiring against us. Everything seems to have been prepared for our sin; the train was laid, and the one little spark fell. Had we had any idea of what was going on we should have been on our guard; had we seen the possible sin, we should have gone out of our way to avoid it. But so suddenly were we set down in presence of the tempting object, that there was scarce a thought of resistance. So wholly at a disadvantage were we taken, that we are inclined to believe that, were we in the same circumstances again, prepared by the same day's pleasure or day's business or night's trouble, instigated by the same company or by the same solitude, brought as suddenly face to face with the same open gate to sin, or driven by the same urgency of motive, freed from the outward restraint that is now upon us, and the reasons on the side of sin equally manifold and thronging, we should now (judging of our own strength from our present experience of it) sin again. And if so, what security have we (who know not what a day may bring forth) against a similar or far more seductive combination of circumstances, except in an appeal to God, whose will orders all things, and whose will is our sanctification?

In this petition, then, we pray directly for this, that God in His consideration of our frailty would so order our life day by day that as little as possible we may be exposed to temptation. But it will be asked, "Has this petition, then, no reference to the temptations we do actually meet? Does it only avert possible temptations, and bring no strength to help us in those that actually occur?" Directly it does not ask from God any such aid. And it seems a profitless exercise of ingenuity, to wrest the words so that they shall include what is evidently included in the second part of the petition, "Deliver us from evil." He who prays these concluding words will surely be little concerned to make the former words mean "bring us out of temptation safely" as well as "lead us not into it." Nevertheless, it must not be overlooked, that this desire, "Lead us not into temptation," has a powerful reflex influence upon the spirit of the petitioner, which enables him, if tempted, to quit himself very differently from what he would otherwise have done. It is a very different war we wage when we have prayed against it, from that we wage, when we have carelessly exposed ourselves. The soldier who is steady in the din and carnage of battle which duty has led him into, will quail and tremble at the little hazards to which a foolish exploit or unadvised adventure has exposed him. If we are engaged in plain duty when temptation assails us, then we can appeal to God for help. And by the acknowledgment of our weakness and fear of sin which is contained in this petition, we do indirectly, but not the less effectually, appeal to the compassion and help of God. If we have asked God to keep us from temptation, and still meet it, then we believe that what we meet is of His ordering, and that good, and not evil, will come of it. Passing through His fire, we are purified. Warring in His warfare, we are rendered more hardy, faithful, and experienced. But if we have not asked His guidance, but have gone forth at our own charges and risks, then how can we with any confidence ask in temptation the help which very probably we should never have needed to ask had we asked God's guidance before? Trying enough it is to fall into temptation after praying, but to fall into it without prayer is a confounding and disastrous thing. It may be good for us to meet temptations, but it is never good to hope for them. It is God's prerogative to lead us into them, for He also (and He only) can bring us through them : it is ours to watch and pray against them, knowing our own weakness. And if any one thinks that by using this petition he resists the providence of God, let him ask himself the simple question, " Do I desire to be tempted ?" If not, then let me pray God to preserve me from temptation. And if, after committing myself to God's care in this matter, I do meet temptations, I shall at least know by whose permission they come, and whose discipline they bring. To view severe temptation as a possible thing, and as a very dangerous thing, this is the best preparation against it.

Out of these words there are continually rising one or two important suggestions of a practical kind. The first is, that we must see to it that we make this an honest request. For it is a pleasant thing to go so far with sin, and break company before its terrible evil is consummated. It is a narrow, but a most attractive path which separates actual, outward transgression from the region whence sin can be contemplated. Few Christians intend to sin, compared to those who only intend to place themselves in dangerous circumstances. There is a pleasure in letting the thoughts dwell on forbidden objects. which provokes us to tamper with sin, and prevents us from resolutely shunning the avenues that lead to evil.   Have I never asked God to deliver me from evil, while a little deeper in my heart there lay the intention of putting myself in the way of temptation without any call ?   To do so is grievously to dishonour God.   It is to expect that He will pander to my evil desires and appetites, that He will suffer me to enjoy the excitement of temptation, and preserve me from the outward disgrace and fully-formed evil of the sin.   It is to take the place of God, and say that it is better I should pray, " Let me so far into temptation," than " Lead me not into it."   And he who cannot comprehend how this should be the one prayer given us concerning the special advancement of our own spirits towards complete redemption, has not yet prayed it as he ought ; is yet, under God's words, hiding his own desires. For this petition goes to the very core of our heart, and tries our real purposes severely ; makes us say, if we are really anxious to be cut off from all chance of sin, all thought of it, and approach to it ; brings us daily to decide whether we should like a state where there was not only no sin, but no temptation. The love of sin is pretty well broken within us, if we can use this petition always and fully; if, considering the persons we shall this day meet, the things that may be said to us, the gratifying offers that may be made to us, the opportunities of pleasure or advancement that may occur, we can yet say, "Rather let me meet none of these than that they should so much as tempt me to evil." Happy indeed is the man who, in the fulness and depth of this petition, can say, "I this day wish to be far from everything which will nourish evil within me, and I desire the presence of such things only as will mature a Christian disposition. I do not desire success, if success is to minister to vain-glory; I do not wish to make money, if money is to minister to covetousness; I do not long for pleasant society, if that is to make me forgetful of God; I do not yearn for leisure, if leisure is to loosen my bond to Jesus Christ." What is this but the entire surrender of our lives to God and for His purposes? What is this but a profession of self-denial, and a resolution to endure all hardness? It is the prayer of a humble and holy spirit; of a spirit at least set on holiness, and knowing that God only can guide us in this life, so that holiness shall be the result. Often it calls us to give up (so far as our own purposes are concerned) prospects of great attraction, but which, we fear, would be adverse to our spiritual growth. We see the beauty of the prospect, it allures us on, but we know not whether the flowers wave and rustle with the healthy breath of heaven or with the subtle windings of the serpent. We will not venture where there may be danger, and where there is not a necessary call, but will pray still to God, "Lead us not thither." And this fear to go where we may offend God, is the same feeling as gives us absolute courage to go wherever we may serve Him.

Another practical hint suggested by this petition is, to shun the beginnings of temptation. It puts us on our guard against the earliest movements of sinward inclination, and prompts us to deal vigorously with its faintest symptoms. All evil is easiest checked in its rise, with less pain to ourselves, and with more unalloyed result. To have parleyed with temptation is to have lost strength already. Go a mile with the tempter, and the chances are that he will persuade you to go two. He will first tell you that you are not

going out of your way at all, and forthwith he
will tell you that you have gone too far to go back.
The first step may not be wrong in itself, but it
is wrong if it be the first of a succession of steps
which lands you in sin. When we find ourselves
very anxious to discover reasons for going on, we
may well suspect whither we are going. We
shall probably find reasons enough, and only after
the sin is committed open our eyes to their hol-
lowness.

It is the former part of this petition which
gives the tone to the latter. The evil we chiefly
aim at being delivered from, is that which comes
of temptation yielded to. Not that the words do
not include every kind of evil, all that man re-
deemed will at last be free from. but the evil
primarily in view here is sin, or what produces
sin. By the words of Christ himself we must
interpret this prayer; and His own petition for
His people is, " I pray not that thou shouldest
take them out of the world, but that thou
shouldest keep them from the evil." Without
being at once put beyond the reach of the
ordinary privations of this life, we may, then, be
delivered from the evil. We can be kept from
the evil without being set above disappointments,

12

sicknesses, distress, loss. We can be delivered from evil without being delivered from this world. This evil, therefore, cannot be in the world so much as in ourselves; cannot be in our condition so much as in our character. All men have an idea that this world has something wrong about it, that our condition here is not altogether satisfying, but to be delivered from. And so we begin to deliver ourselves, and set to work at the outmost branches of evil instead of at the root; we provide against loss, guard against disease, while we ought to be asking God to deliver us from that evil which is within us, and which, though all these outer branches of evil were lopped off, would send forth fresh branches; which, though we were put into a world where all was blessed, and well-ordered, and according to the best, would soon spoil that world as it has spoiled this. It was by yielding to temptation we ever became connected with evil of any kind; first with evil doing, and then with all other evil. Through the heart of man did evil steal its way into this world. And until it be expelled from the heart, it will find its way into all we are connected with. Could there be a fairer world than this was when God pronounced it very good, and "when the morning stars sang together, and all the sons of God shouted for joy?" Take from this world all that sin has wrought, and you shall have a world fairer than your imagination, though not than God's purpose, can conceive. No doubt we inherit a troop of evils, and fall heirs to the ills that men have been aggravating from the first, but there is that in each one of us which, if we be not delivered from it, will turn the happiest and most faultless inheritance into sorrow and confusion. Our evil dispositions do not show all their deadly influence now, only because what they would do is done already. They do not destroy the world, because the world is already destroyed.

And appalling as are the effects of the "one man's disobedience," and of that whereby all his descendants have ratified his act and approved their parentage, more appalling still is it to find the hold and the power that sin has over us. Many of the effects of sin, and especially those of them which are most palpable to us here, spend their force and pass away. That effect of sin which admonishes us of a sinful future, the helplessness and bondage of sin, that effect of sin which is sin itself, is the most alarming of its

present results. We see no prospect of accidental deliverance from this, nor of its merely
wearing out. With sin the law of age is re-
versed; and time, which weakens and consumes
all else, adds vigour and life to sin. And yet
there is hope, near and bright. However mul-
tiplied, involved, deep-rooted, or grievous be our
sinful propensities, there is a deliverance out of
them all. There is a deliverance from all their
effects; but we can readily believe this, yes, and
patiently wait for it, when we find that there is a
deliverance from our sinful natures themselves.
And this God has wrought, and now works, in all
them that pray this prayer; for " God has raised
up his Son Jesus, and sent him to bless you, in
turning away every one of you from his iniquities." It is He who " delivers us, and doth deliver, in whom we trust that He will yet deliver."
Therefore will our hearts together praise Him.
and our own joy will dictate these words, " Thine
is the kingdom, the glory, and the power. for
ever. Amen "